Mich Turner's
CAKE MASTERCLASS

Mich Turner's
CAKE MASTERCLASS

The Ultimate Guide to Cake Decorating Perfection

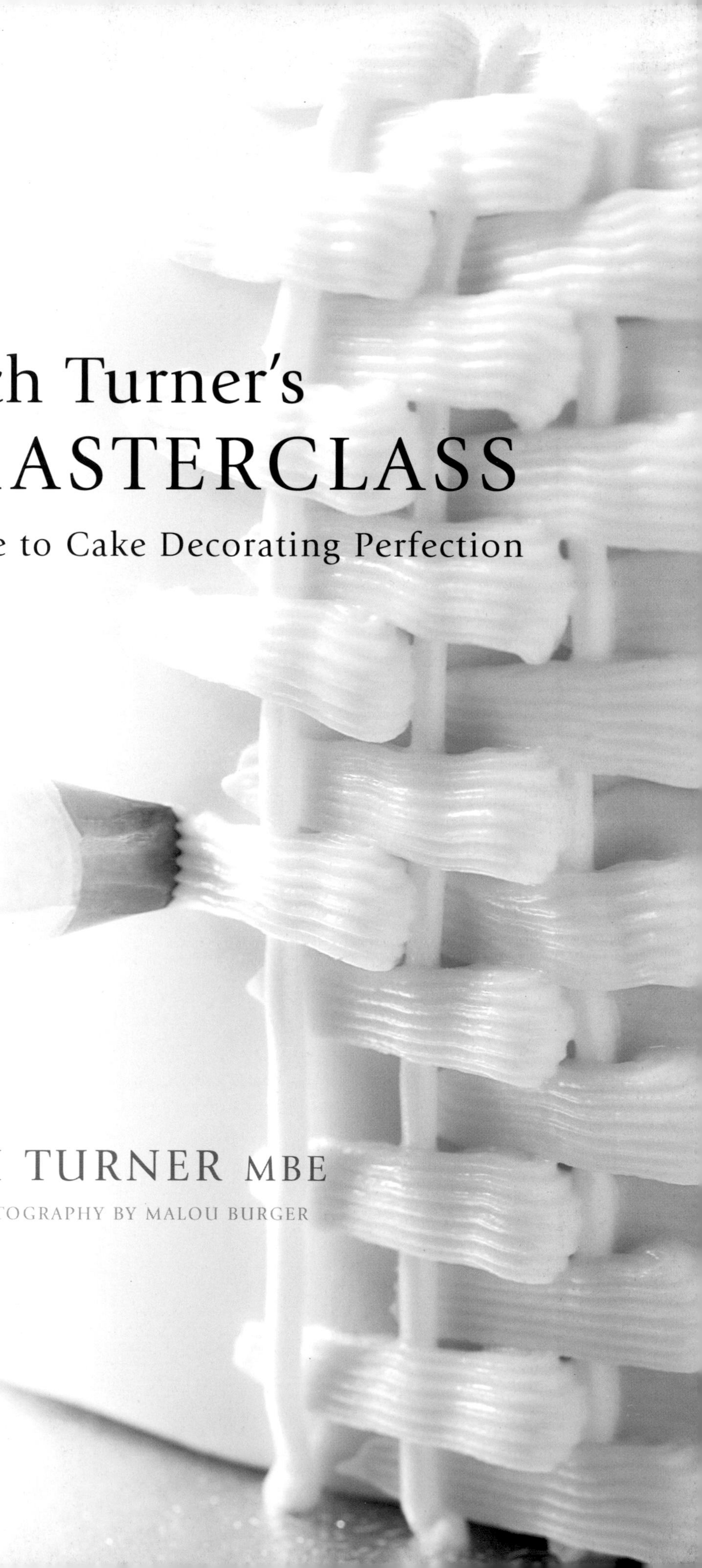

MICH TURNER MBE

WITH PHOTOGRAPHY BY MALOU BURGER

jacqui
small

DEDICATION
For Marvellous Marlow and Gorgeous George, with love

Publisher's note: This book includes some recipes containing raw eggs and nuts.
It is advisable for more vulnerable people such as pregnant or nursing mothers,
invalids and the elderly and those with known allergic reactions to avoid dishes
made with these ingredients.

First published in 2011 by
Jacqui Small Llp
An imprint of Aurum Press Ltd
7 Greenland Street
London NW1 0ND

Text copyright © Mich Turner 2011
Photography, design and layout copyright © Jacqui Small 2011

The author's moral rights have been asserted.

Publisher: Jacqui Small
Managing Editor: Kerenza Swift
Editor: Alison Bolus
Art Director: Ashley Western
Production: Peter Colley

ISBN: 978 1 906417 96 3

A catalogue record for this book is available from the British Library.

2013 2012
10 9 8 7 6 5

Printed in China

Contents

Welcome to my Masterclass. In this book I will give you the tools, techniques and tips required to introduce you to the world of perfect cake making, baking and decorating. Whether you are looking to learn a new skill as a complete novice, increase your repertoire as a keen decorator or enhance your skills as a semi-professional, I hope this book will encourage, inspire and tutor you effectively to create some amazing cakes.

We start with Essential Equipment, which identifies the specialist tools you will need, followed by Cake Baking, which contains many methods to guarantee perfect results. Try them out to find your favourites.

In Fillings and Frostings, I give you a number of recipes you can use to fill and frost your cakes, from a simple afternoon teatime cake to a luxury pudding.

Careful Covering and Stacking will show you how to cover and stack your cakes flawlessly, pointing out many of the potential pitfalls to avoid to ensure you have the perfect cake all ready for additional decoration.

The Masterclass section will show you in detail how to achieve many of the techniques I use in everyday cake decorating, from hand piping, painting and moulding to using cutters and ribbons.

Finally, the Cake Gallery is where the inspiration comes alive, as many of the techniques from the masterclass are put into practice.

My aim has been to provide you with a comprehensive manual of cake decorating. I am sure this could lead to several volumes....

Be inspired!

Paint palette for
mixing colour

Colour dusts

Paintbrushes

Nozzles in various sizes and shapes

Assorted flower petal cutters

Concentric round cutters

Smiley tool

Small ball tool

Large ball tool

Pokey tool

Shell / marking tool

Retractable pokey tool

Assorted ribbons – grosgrain, double satin and organza in plain and patterned versions

Edible glitter

Flower plunger cutters

Essential Equipment

Daffodil cutter

Heart metal cutter

Ribbon insertion tools

Daffodil cutter

Tools of the Trade

A skilled craftsman requires professional tools to carry out their work, and baking and decorating cakes are no exception. Invest in a reliable set of kitchen scales, ideally digital for accuracy. Mixing bowls can be glass, plastic or stainless steel, but ensure you have some in different sizes: large, roomy bowls for aerating, creaming and whisking, and smaller bowls for melting chocolate and weighing ingredients.

Cake-making equipment

Hand-held balloon whisks (a), electric whisks (b) and larger table-top mixers are all useful for mixing larger quantities or for more controlled precision work for cakes, fillings and frostings.

I like to use good-quality, sturdy tins to bake my cakes (c, d), whether plain or more fancy. Tins will remain rigid and are a good heat conductor, so are perfect for tiered cakes. Silicone moulds are also good for the interestingly shaped cakes they create. The moulds, which are now

widely available, are non-stick and versatile enough to be used safely in the oven, freezer, microwave and dishwasher.

Wire cooling racks (e) are essential for cooling large and small cakes, and for holding cakes to be covered in poured chocolate ganache. Finally, sieves and tea strainers in various sizes (f, g) are useful for many tasks, such as sifting flour or dusting a cake or work surface with icing sugar or cocoa powder.

Lining a tin

All cake tins need to be lined to protect the outer surfaces of the cake during the baking time. The technique is similar for a round or square tin.

1 Cut 2 sheets of non-stick baking parchment, either round or square, just a little smaller than the base of the tin. Brush the inside of the tin with melted butter or sunflower oil

and place one liner in the bottom. Fold a long sheet of non-stick baking parchment in half lengthways, then fold the long folded edge up by 12mm (½in). Use a sharp pair of scissors to snip diagonally at 2.5cm (1in) intervals from the first folded edge to the second fold.

2 Place the collar inside the tin, pushing the diagonal cut edge to fit

neatly. Brush over the cut edge with melted butter or sunflower oil. Trim the top edge of the collar so that it protrudes no higher than 2.5cm (1in) above the height of the tin.

3 Place the second non-stick baking paper liner in the base of the tin to cover the cut bottom edge of the paper collar. The tin is now ready to be used.

a Large silicone rolling pin
b Pizza wheel
c Palette knife
d Serrated knife
e Small sharp knife
f Spatula
g Small silicone rolling pin
h Wooden spoon
i Pastry brush
j Icing smoothers
k Non-slip turntable

Cake-filling, covering and decorating equipment

A large serrated knife can be used to split cakes, and a selection of palette knives is useful to spread buttercreams and cream cheese frostings.

Use concentric metal cutters (see p.8) in three sizes for cutting out what you need for individual cakes: one for the cake, one for the base coat and one for the top coat.

I like to use silicone rolling pins for rolling out marzipan, sugar paste and chocolate plastique. Silicone retains its temperature and gives the paste a smooth, even finish, unlike marble, which can chill the paste, or wood, which can impart a grain-like texture. Rolling pins come in various sizes: larger pins for rolling out sheets of marzipan and smaller pins for feathering chocolate plastique collars and petal paste for models or flowers.

Pizza wheels are great for cutting pastes. Being a rotary cutter, a pizza wheel will not snag or pull the pastes.

Moulded plastic icing smoothers are essential for a flawless finish, to achieve the smoothest coverings of marzipan, sugar paste and chocolate plastique. Invest in one moulded-edged smoother for the tops of cakes and two straight-edged smoothers for the sides or for working on individual cakes.

Set cakes on a non-slip turntable for ease of decorating. A 20cm (8in) size turntable is good for most individual cakes and single tiers, and a 35cm (14in) lower turntable is perfect for working on stacked and tiered cakes.

Your professional kit should also include: a selection of stainless-steel piping nozzles, non-stick piping bags in different sizes, various paintbrushes, colour dusts, colour pastes, metallic lustres, cocoa butter, dipping alcohol, edible varnish, cutters and modelling tools, including a ball tool. In addition, you will need three pairs of scissors: small precision scissors for ribbon, larger, general-purpose scissors for templates and a heavy-duty pair for dowelling rods. You will also need a pokey tool, fine-liner pen and non-toxic pencil for transferring the template designs.

There are so many pretty, stylish cake stands and plates available in different sizes and shapes. I collect them whenever I see them – glass, fine porcelain, chunky china, hand painted, laser cut – you can never have too many to serve so many beautiful, fun or stylish cakes.

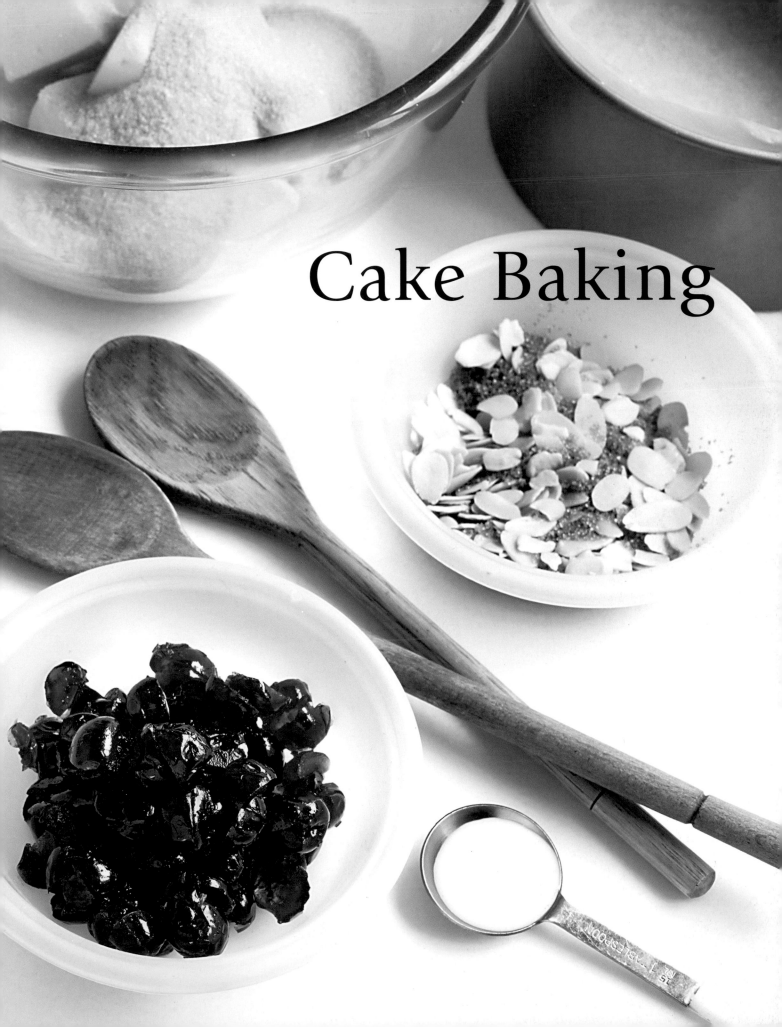

Cake Baking

There are several methods of cake making, resulting in different-style cakes. In this chapter I will show and explain the basic methods, which include creaming, melting, all-in-one and whisking, plus provide you with lots of delicious recipes. Some cakes have a delicious filling or frosting and are perfect for serving for afternoon tea, whereas others are more suited to being used as a base for covering and decorating. There are also those that are versatile enough to be considered for either. I will identify these where they are included in this chapter. As a rule of thumb, all ingredients should be at room temperature unless otherwise stated. I like to use unrefined sugars, organic flours, organic free-range eggs, 70% cocoa solids plain chocolate and fresh fruits for zesting.

Creaming

Cakes made by the creaming method rely on precise measurements, all the ingredients being at room temperature and the mixture being beaten well at each stage. They also need to have air incorporated at each of the beating stages to result in a well-risen cake, with even texture and a clean bite. The cake should not be dense or crumbly.

Beat the butter and sugar together until really light and fluffy. This should be done with an electric whisk and will take 10 minutes. If you do not have an electric whisk, you will have to use a wooden spoon and beat for a long time!

The eggs should be beaten together before being added a little at a time, with the whisk still beating, to prevent the mixture curdling (separating). If the mixture does separate, simply add a spoonful of flour and continue beating in the egg. It will not ruin the cake, but the texture will be a little more dense.

Sift the flour in and fold it into the mixture carefully with a metal spoon, to avoid breaking down the air bubbles that were created during the beating stages.

Stir in any final ingredients, then transfer the mixture to the tin carefully, to preserve as much air as possible.

Melting

Cakes made by the melting method are the most reliable and so are perfect for beginners. They rely on the addition of a strong raising agent (bicarbonate of soda), rather than the inclusion of air, to raise the cake.

Melt the sugar and butter or oil together, then combine this liquid with the eggs. Stir the dry ingredients into the mixture before transferring it to the tin. Bicarbonate of soda has a distinctive taste, so spices such as ginger, cinnamon and nutmeg are often added to these cakes to mask the flavour. These cakes tend to be very moist, but are more dense in texture than other cakes.

All-in-one

For all-in-one cakes, the ingredients must be at room temperature and accurately weighed. The method is as simple as it sounds: you put all the ingredients into a bowl and beat them together with an electric whisk (or a wooden spoon, if you don't have a whisk) until they are well combined. In addition to using self-raising flour, you will need to add another raising agent (in this case baking powder). Baking powder is a gentler raising agent than bicarbonate of soda, because although it does contain some bicarbonate of soda, it is blended with cream of tartar, which counterbalances the harsh flavour. These cakes will have a similar, but more dense, texture to the creamed cakes.

TIP It is important to use fresh self-raising flour and baking power, as their potency does fade over time.

Whisking

Whisked cakes have very little, if any, fat in them, relying instead on air being incorporated when the eggs and sugar are whisked together. These cakes are incredibly light and airy, making them a good choice following a heavy meal, but must be eaten on the day they are made as they will dry out quickly, having no butter or oil to keep them moist.

Whisked cakes will generally be accompanied by a cream- or butter-based filling, frosting or topping to introduce a fat content to keep them moist and balance the taste and texture.

Again, all ingredients should be at room temperature. Whisk the eggs and sugar until they are really pale and thick, which can take 10 minutes even with an electric whisk. Stir in all the other ingredients carefully to avoid breaking down the air bubbles.

Cherry and Almond Cake

Creaming • Cherries and almonds go together beautifully in this light yet moist cake. Although the cake is delicious on its own, I've added a sweet crunchy topping of some demerara sugar and flaked almonds, which makes it that extra bit special! This cake keeps well and can be used as the base for a decorated celebration cake if it is baked without the crunchy topping. The photographs highlight the key stages involved in the creaming method. Do not be tempted to rush any of these stages, and ensure all the ingredients are at room temperature.

- 225g (8oz) unsalted butter, plus extra for greasing
- 225g (8oz) golden caster sugar
- 4 large eggs, lightly beaten
- 225g (8oz) plain flour
- ½ tsp baking powder
- 115g (4oz) ground almonds
- 250g (9oz) naturally coloured glacé cherries, quartered
- 1 tsp almond extract
- 1 tbsp milk
- 2 tbsp demerara sugar
- 2 tbsp flaked almonds

- bake: fan 160°C (325°F)
- conventional 180°C (350°F) gas mark 4

1 Preheat the oven. Put the butter and sugar in a bowl.

2 Start beating them together.

3 Continue beating until the mixture is light, pale and fluffy.

4 Gradually beat in the eggs, a little at a time.

5 Sift the flour and baking powder into the bowl.

6 Carefully fold into the creamed mixture, using a metal spoon.

7 Add the ground almonds.

8 Add the glacé cherries, almond extract and milk.

9 Carefully fold into the mixture.

10 Spoon the cake mixture into a 20cm (8in) greased and lined cake tin.

11 Level off the top with the back of a spoon.

12 Sprinkle with the demerara sugar and flaked almonds.

13 This will form the crunchy topping when the cake is cooked.

14 Bake the cake in the centre of the oven for 1 hour, then cover with foil and continue cooking for a further 15–20 minutes, or until the cake has shrunk away from the sides of the tin, the centre is springy to touch and a skewer inserted into the middle of the cake comes out clean. Leave the cake to cool in the tin for 15 minutes before turning it out on to a wire rack to cool completely.

*TO STORE Store in a tin or wrapped in greaseproof paper or foil for up to 1 week. Alternatively, wrap the cake in a double layer of greaseproof paper and aluminium foil and place in the freezer for up to 1 month.

Madagascan Berry Vanilla Cake

Creaming • For a truly authentic flavour, it is imperative to use seeds from vanilla pods to make this cake. The addition of Greek-style yogurt in the mixture gives the cake a lovely texture, and the cake is finished off with a creamy berry topping.

For the cake:
- 250g (9oz) unsalted butter, plus extra for greasing
- 250g (9oz) golden caster sugar
- seeds from 1 vanilla pod
- 5 large eggs, lightly beaten
- 85g (3¼oz) plain flour
- 250g (9oz) self-raising flour
- 100g (3½oz) full-fat Greek-style coconut yogurt
- 3 tbsp milk
- 100g (3½oz) raspberries
- 100g (3½oz) blueberries

For the topping:
- 250ml (9fl oz) crème fraîche
- 50g (2oz) raspberries
- 50g (2oz) blueberries

- bake: fan 160°C (325°F)
- conventional 180°C (350°F) gas mark 4

1 Preheat the oven. Grease and line a deep 20cm (8in) cake tin with non-stick baking paper or use a non-stick cake tin. Ensure all the ingredients are at room temperature. Beat the butter, sugar and vanilla seeds together until they are light and fluffy (a).

2 Add the eggs a little at a time, beating well after each addition. If the mixture starts to curdle, stir in 1 tablespoon of one of the flours. Beat in the yogurt. Sift the flours together and fold into the creamed mixture, followed by the milk. Spoon half the mixture into the base of the prepared cake tin and stir the raspberries and blueberries into the remainder (b). Spoon this mixture on top of the bottom layer and bake in the oven for 1 hour 20 minutes.

3 Remove the cake from the oven and leave to cool a little on a wire rack, then turn out and leave to cool completely. To serve, spoon the crème fraîche onto the top of the cake and dress with the raspberries and blueberries (c).

Note that this cake can settle and sink slightly overnight. It can therefore be a good idea to dowel tiers made using this recipe as close to the time of stacking or blocking as possible (see pp.82–3), to ensure the cake is stable.

*TO STORE With no filling or topping, this cake will keep for 7 days wrapped in greaseproof paper or covered with marzipan and icing or chocolate. Alternatively, wrap the cake in a double layer of greaseproof paper and aluminium foil and place in the freezer for up to 1 month. This recipe is perfect to use as a base for a decorated celebration cake. Once the cake is filled and covered, it must be refrigerated and eaten on the day.

Chocolate Truffle Torte

Creaming • This cake, which is rich but not too sweet, is made with melted chocolate, so the texture is similar to that of a chocolate brownie. As there is comparatively very little flour, the recipe relies on the chocolate and eggs to support the finished cake. It can be covered with marzipan and icing, then decorated, or covered in chocolate ganache and served with fresh berries as a dessert. For a deep cake, you should split the mixture between two 7.5cm- (3in-) deep cake tins (so the cake cooks evenly whilst retaining a good height), then sandwich together with buttercream. For a single-depth cake, just one of the cakes is used. Individual small cakes can be stamped out of a single-depth cake (see pp.66 and 69).

a

1 Preheat the oven. Grease and line 2 deep cake tins of the correct size with non-stick baking paper or use non-stick cake tins. Ensure all the ingredients are at room temperature. Melt the chocolate in a microwave or in a bowl over simmering water, then allow to cool.

2 Beat the butter and sugar together until light and fluffy. Beat in the eggs a little at a time, beating well between each addition. Pour the chocolate in slowly (a), beating all the time. Stir in the vanilla extract, then fold in the flour.

3 Spoon the mixture evenly into the 2 prepared cake tins and bake for the time stated. The cakes should be well risen, with a crust, but will still wobble when shaken gently. Remove from the oven and leave to cool before turning out. The crust will sink back onto the cake – this is normal.

4 If decorating this cake, sandwich the 2 halves together with buttercream. For added luxury, slice each half horizontally and sandwich again.

*TO STORE This cake will keep for up to 10 days once covered and decorated or wrapped in greaseproof paper and kept in an airtight container. Although it can be refrigerated if prepared in advance with fresh fruit, allow time for it to come up to room temperature to ensure the melted chocolate in the recipe adds to the truffle texture. It is suitable for freezing. Defrost overnight.

TIP Be careful not to overbake this cake, as it can become dry and crumbly.

FOR THE CAKE (round/square)	15cm (6in)	20cm (8in)/15cm (6in)	25cm (10in)/20cm (8in)	30cm (12in)/25cm (10in)
plain chocolate (70% cocoa solids) broken into pieces and melted	200g (7oz)	400g (14oz)	600g (1lb 5oz)	800g (1lb 12oz)
unsalted butter, plus extra for greasing	250g (9oz)	500g (1lb 2oz)	750g (1lb 10oz)	1kg (2lb 4oz)
light brown sugar	350g (12oz)	700g (1lb 9oz)	1.05kg (2lb 5oz)	1.4kg (3lb 2oz)
medium eggs, lightly beaten	5	10	15	20
vanilla extract	1½ tsp	1 tbsp	4½ tsp	2 tbsp
plain flour, sifted	140g (5oz)	280g (10oz)	420g (15oz)	550g (1lb 4oz)
bake: fan 140°C (275°F) conventional 160°C (325°F) gas mark 3	45 minutes	1 hour	1 hour 20 minutes	1 hour 40 minutes

Chocolate and Cherry Cake

Creaming • This is the ultimate indulgent chocolate cake. French glacé cherries are soaked in vintage port overnight, which gives this cake a wonderful richness and delicious flavour. Serve for pudding or a special afternoon tea, covered in smooth poured dark chocolate ganache.

a

For the cake:
- 250g (9oz) unsalted butter, plus extra for greasing
- 200g (7oz) plain chocolate (70% cocoa solids)
- 350g (12oz) light brown sugar
- 5 medium eggs
- 1 tsp vanilla extract
- 100g (3½oz) whole French glacé cherries, soaked overnight in 5 tbsp vintage port
- 140g (5oz) plain flour

For the topping:
- ½ quantity chocolate ganache buttercream (see p.53), at room temperature
- 1 quantity chocolate ganache (see p.50)
- 225g (8oz) fresh cherries

- bake: fan 140°C (275°F)
- conventional 160°C (325°F) gas mark 3

1 Preheat the oven. Grease and line a deep 20cm (8in) round cake tin with non-stick baking paper or use a non-stick cake tin. Ensure all the ingredients are at room temperature.

2 Melt the chocolate in a bowl over a pan of just-boiled water or in a microwave and leave to cool.

3 Beat the butter and sugar together in a mixing bowl until light and fluffy. Add the eggs, one at a time, until they are all incorporated. Pour in the melted chocolate, beating all the time, then stir in the vanilla extract (a). Finally, add the cherries with any remaining port. Sift the flour into the mixture and fold in gently.

4 Spoon the mixture into the prepared tin and bake for 55–60 minutes. Leave to cool in the tin, then turn out on to a wire rack.

5 Following the instructions on p.51 for pouring ganache, cover the top and sides with a thin coat of buttercream and chill in the fridge for 15 minutes. When the cake is covered in ganache, use a palette knife to make waves on the top and to smooth the sides.

6 Leave the ganache to set for 10 minutes, before using a small knife to lever the cake from the rack and trim the base edge. Meanwhile, gather up the remaining ganache from under the wire rack and put it in a bowl. Once it has cooled a little and thickened, spoon it into a piping bag fitted with a star nozzle, ready to pipe.

7 Place the cake on a decorative stand. Pipe scrolls around the top edge of the cake in an alternating pattern, as shown, pulling each scroll to a tail before starting the next.

8 For the shells around the base, pipe a uniform trail with the ganache. Dress the cake with the fresh cherries.

TIP If the ganache firms up and becomes too stiff to pipe, remove and gently reheat and allow to cool again until it reaches the desired consistency.

*TO STORE Store this cake at room temperature and eat within 2 days. Alternatively, wrap the cake in a double layer of greaseproof paper and aluminium foil and place in the freezer for up to 1 month.

Luscious Lemon Cake

Creaming • This has to be the supreme lemon cake. It is deliciously moist, fresh and so lemony it never fails to impress. Serve it with a simple lemon curd buttercream or use it as a base covered with marzipan, sugar paste or chocolate plastique for a special celebration cake. Be sure to weigh the ingredients accurately, have them at room temperature and ensure each stage is well creamed or beaten before moving on to the next step.

a

1 Grease and line the cake tin with non-stick baking paper or use a non-stick cake tin. Ensure all the ingredients are at room temperature. Place the butter and sugar in a clean bowl and beat with an electric whisk until light and fluffy. Add the rest of the ingredients and mix to a fairly runny cake mixture.

2 Transfer the mixture into the prepared tin and bake for the relevant time, or until a skewer inserted into the middle of the cake comes out clean.

3 As soon as you have put the cake into the oven, combine the lemon juice and sugar for the syrup glaze in a bowl and leave until the sugar has completely dissolved.

4 Remove the cake from the oven and use a skewer to spike holes all over the cake, ensuring you reach all the way to the bottom. Pour the syrup over the cake and leave until the cake has absorbed it and is cool. Turn out onto a wire rack, cut into three layers and fill with lemon curd buttercream (see p.52). Dust the top with icing sugar.

Note that this cake can settle and sink slightly overnight. It can therefore be a good idea to dowel tiers made using this recipe as close to the time of stacking or blocking as possible, to ensure the cake is stable.

FOR THE CAKE	15cm (6in) round	20cm (8in) round/ 15cm (6in) square	25cm (10in) round/ 20cm (8in) square	30cm (12in) round/ 25cm (10in) square
unsalted butter, plus extra for greasing	175g (6oz)	350g (12oz)	525g (1lb 3oz)	700g (1lb 9oz)
golden caster sugar	175g (6oz)	350g (12oz)	525g (1lb 3oz)	700g (1lb 9oz)
self-raising flour	175g (6oz)	350g (12oz)	525g (1lb 3oz)	700g (1lb 9oz)
baking powder	1 tsp	2 tsp	1 tbsp	4 tsp
medium eggs, lightly beaten	3	6	9	12
finely grated lemon zest	2 lemons	4 lemons	6 lemons	8 lemons
milk	5 tbsp	150ml (5fl oz)	225ml (7½fl oz)	300ml (10fl oz)
vanilla extract	1 tsp	2 tsp	1 tbsp	4 tsp
FOR THE SYRUP GLAZE				
lemon juice	2 lemons	4 lemons	6 lemons	8 lemons
granulated sugar	75g (3oz)	150g (5½oz)	225g (8oz)	300g (10½oz)
bake: fan 160°C (325°F) conventional 180°C (350°F) gas mark 4	55 minutes	1 hour 10 minutes	1½ hours	1¾ hours

Polly's Sticky Ginger Cake

Melting • There is nothing quite like the smell, let alone the taste, of a ginger cake. Warm, rich and spicy, it is the ideal cake for a winter's afternoon tea by the fire. Because this cake is made by the melting method, you need to start off with some of the ingredients in a saucepan, but once they are melted you can pour them into a mixing bowl and stir in the remaining ingredients, just as you would for a cake made by the creaming method. The resulting texture will be moist and sticky, as every good ginger cake should be.

- 125g (4½oz) unsalted butter, plus extra for greasing
- 300g (10½oz) dark muscovado sugar
- 2 eggs
- 100ml (3½fl oz) milk
- 250g (9oz) plain flour
- 1 tbsp ground ginger
- 1 tsp bicarbonate of soda
- 100g (3½oz) preserved stem ginger, finely chopped, plus 3 tbsp of the syrup

- bake: fan 160°C (325°F)
- conventional 180°C (350°F) gas mark 4

a

b

c

1 Preheat the oven. Grease and line a deep 900g (2lb) loaf tin with non-stick baking paper or use a non-stick loaf tin. Ensure all the ingredients are at room temperature.

2 Put the butter and sugar into a large pan and melt over a low heat. Remove from the heat, pour into a mixing bowl and stir well (a).

3 Add the eggs and milk and beat well (b). Sift the flour, ground ginger and bicarbonate of soda into the bowl (c).

4 Add the stem ginger and syrup and stir well to combine, breaking up any lumps of flour (d).

5 Pour the mixture into the prepared tin and bake for 1 hour or until a skewer inserted into the middle of the cake comes out clean. Leave the cake to cool in the tin for 5 minutes, then turn out. Peel off the lining paper and leave to cool on a wire rack.

*TO STORE Store in a tin or wrapped in greaseproof paper or foil for up to 1 week. Alternatively, wrap in greaseproof paper and foil and freeze for up to 1 month.

TIP Bicarbonate of soda reacts once it makes contact with liquid, so put the cake in the oven as soon as it is mixed.

d

Rich Fruit Celebration Cake

Melting • This fruit cake is tried and tested as being the best ever! This recipe revolutionises other rich fruit cake recipes as it is made, rather unusually, by melting the butter and sugar together first, then stirring in all the delicious plump vine fruits that have been steeping in brandy for hours. This ensures the cake is really moist and fruity and bakes to give a dense, even result, whilst at the same time remaining flat on the top, which makes it perfect for using as a base for decorating. It is delicious on its own or can be covered in the traditional combination of marzipan and icing.

a

1 Grease and line a deep cake tin with non-stick baking paper or use a non-stick cake tin. Wash the fruits and drain through a sieve. Tip into a bowl, and pour the brandy over the mixture. Leave to steep for up to 6 hours.

2 Preheat the oven. Ensure all the ingredients are at room temperature. Melt the butter and sugar together in a saucepan, stirring until well mixed, then pour into a mixing bowl. Add the treacle and mix well, then add the eggs and mix again. Sift in the flour, baking powder and spices and fold in well, then stir in the steeped fruit and remaining liquid, the glacé ginger and vanilla extract (a).

3 Spoon the mixture into the prepared tin and bake until a skewer inserted into the middle of the cake comes out clean. Leave the cake to cool in the tin and turn out when cold.

*TO STORE Wrap in a double layer of greaseproof paper and a layer of foil. Store at room temperature to mature for up to 6 weeks prior to the event. Once covered in marzipan and icing, this cake will keep for a further 6 months at room temperature. Alternatively, store in the freezer wrapped in a double layer of greaseproof paper and double layer of foil pretty much indefinitely.

FOR THE CAKE	15cm (6in) round or square	20cm (8in) round or square	25cm (10in) round or square	30cm (12in) round or square
unsalted butter, plus extra for greasing	125g (4½oz)	250g (9oz)	375g (13oz)	500g (1lb 2oz)
naturally coloured glacé cherries, halved	180g (6½oz)	360g (12½oz)	540g (1lb 3½oz)	720g (1lb 9½oz)
sultanas	160g (6oz)	320g (11oz)	480g (1lb 1oz)	640g (1lb 7oz)
raisins	225g (8oz)	450g (1lb)	675g (1lb 8oz)	900g (2lh)
currants	280g (10oz)	550g (1lb 4oz)	830g (1lb 13oz)	1.1kg (2lb 7oz)
brandy	115ml (3¾fl oz)	225ml (7½fl oz)	340ml (11½fl oz)	450ml (16fl oz)
dark muscovado sugar	125g (4½oz)	260g (9½oz)	385g (13½oz)	520g (1lb 3oz)
treacle	½ tbsp	1 tbsp	1½ tbsp	2 tbsp
eggs, lightly beaten	3 medium	5 large	5 large + 3 medium	10 large
plain flour	120g (4½oz)	240g (8½oz)	360g (12¾oz)	480g (1lb 1oz)
baking powder	¼ tsp	½ tsp	¾ tsp	1 tsp
ground cinnamon	¼ tsp	½ tsp	¾ tsp	1 tsp
ground ginger	¼ tsp	½ tsp	¾ tsp	1 tsp
ground nutmeg	¼ tsp	½ tsp	¾ tsp	1 tsp
ground cloves	⅛ tsp	¼ tsp	⅜ tsp	½ tsp
mixed spice	¼ tsp	½ tsp	¾ tsp	1 tsp
glacé ginger	20g (¾oz)	40g (1½oz)	60g (2½oz)	80g (2¾oz)
vanilla extract	¼ tsp	½ tsp	¾ tsp	1 tsp
bake: fan 120°C (250°F) conventional 140°C (275°F) gas mark 1	2 hours	2½ hours	3 hours	3½ hours

- 200g (7oz) unsalted butter, cut into pieces, plus extra for greasing
- 240g (8½oz) Medjool dates, stoned
- 50g (2oz) sultanas
- 300g (10½oz) light brown sugar
- 2 eggs, lightly beaten
- 25g (1oz) preserved stem ginger, chopped
- grated zest of 2 lemons
- 1 tsp vanilla extract
- 250g (9oz) Bramley cooking apples, peeled and cored, then grated or chopped
- 200g (7oz) plain flour
- ½ tsp baking powder

bake: fan 150°C (300°F)
conventional 170°C (325°F) gas mark 3

Queen Elizabeth Date Cake

Melting • Moist and tasty, this nutritious cake is sustaining and simple to make, and it turns out well every time. It can be covered with marzipan and sugar paste and decorated for an impressive centrepiece, or simply enjoyed on its own served with English breakfast tea or some freshly brewed coffee.

1 Preheat the oven. Grease and line a deep 15cm (6in) round cake tin or 900g (2lb) loaf tin with non-stick baking paper, or use a non-stick tin. Ensure all the ingredients are at room temperature.

2 Place the dates and sultanas in a bowl and cover with boiling water. Melt the butter and light brown sugar together in a saucepan and leave to cool slightly. Beat the eggs, ginger, lemon zest and vanilla extract into the butter and sugar. Drain the fruit and chop the dates finely. Add to the saucepan with the apples and mix well. Sift in the flour and baking powder and fold in well.

3 Spoon the mixture into the tin and bake in the oven for about 1¼ hours until well risen and a skewer inserted into the middle of the cake comes out clean. Leave to cool in the tin.

*TO STORE This cake lasts for 1 week if wrapped in greaseproof paper and aluminium foil and stored in an airtight container. Alternatively, wrap the cake in a double layer of greaseproof paper and aluminium foil and place in the freezer for up to 1 month. It is delicious if kept in the fridge and served cold.

Moist Carrot Cake

Melting • This carrot cake recipe is universally adored. It is made with oil rather than butter, which puts it into the melted category of cakes, so results are pretty much guaranteed! It is a lighter alternative to a rich fruit cake but still very fruity, zesty and spicy. It is baked with walnuts, rum-soaked sultanas and coconut. Once the cake is baked, it is spiked with a fresh citrus syrup, which helps to keep the cake moist. This cake is baked without dairy products, so is suitable for people with a dairy intolerance. It isn't necessary to add a filling or topping – but for a special celebration, fill the cake with a layer of orange buttercream (see p.52) prior to covering with marzipan and icing and decorating the cake. Alternatively, for a teatime treat, top the cake with some orange cream cheese frosting (see p.56) and decorate with some chopped walnuts.

FOR THE CAKE (round/square)	15cm (6in)	20cm (8in)/15cm (6in)	25cm (10in)/20cm (8in)	30cm (12in)/25cm (10in)
sunflower oil, plus extra for greasing	150ml (5fl oz)	300ml (10fl oz)	450ml (16fl oz)	600ml (1 pint)
dark rum	25ml (1fl oz)	50ml (2fl oz)	75ml (2½fl oz)	100ml (3½fl oz)
sultanas	100g (3½oz)	200g (7oz)	300g (10½oz)	400g (14oz)
plain flour	175g (6oz)	350g (12oz)	525g (1lb 3oz)	750g (1lb 10oz)
ground cinnamon	2 tsp	4 tsp	2 tbsp	8 tsp
ground nutmeg	1 tsp	2 tsp	1 tbsp	4 tsp
bicarbonate of soda	1 tsp	2 tsp	1 tbsp	4 tsp
golden caster sugar	75g (3oz)	150g (5½oz)	225g (8oz)	300g (10½oz)
light brown sugar	75g (3oz)	150g (5½oz)	225g (8oz)	300g (10½oz)
medium eggs	2	4	6	8
lemon zest	1	2	3	4
orange zest	1	2	3	4
carrots, peeled and grated	175g (6oz)	350g (12oz)	525g (1lb 3oz)	700g (1lb 9oz)
desiccated coconut	50g (2oz)	100g (3½oz)	150g (5½oz)	200g (7oz)
Californian walnuts, chopped	50g (2oz)	100g (3½oz)	150g (5½oz)	200g (7oz)
vanilla extract	1 tsp	2 tsp	1 tbsp	4 tsp
glacé ginger, chopped (optional)	2 tsp	1 tbsp	4½ tsp	2 tbsp
FOR THE CITRUS SYRUP				
lemon(s), juiced	1	2	2	3
orange(s), juiced	1	1	2	2
light brown sugar	75g (3oz)	110g (3¾oz)	150g (5½oz)	225g (8oz)
bake: fan 130°C (260°F) conventional 150°C (300°F) gas mark 3	1½ hours	2 hours	2½ hours	3 hours

a

b

1 Grease and line a deep cake tin of the correct size with non-stick baking paper or use a non-stick cake tin. Ensure all the ingredients are at room temperature (a). Pour the rum over the sultanas and leave to infuse for 1 hour.

2 Preheat the oven. Sift the flour together with the spices and the bicarbonate of soda. Beat together the sugars, sunflower oil and eggs until smooth. Stir the spiced flour into the smooth mixture, then add the remaining ingredients (including the glacé ginger, if using) and stir well.

3 Spoon the mixture into the prepared tin and bake for the time stated or until a skewer inserted into the middle of the cake comes out clean.

4 Make the syrup while the cake is baking. Strain the juices into a jug, add the sugar and stir well. Continue to stir at intervals while the cake is in the oven. As soon as the cake is out of the oven, pierce it with a skewer several times (b), then carefully spoon or pour the citrus syrup over the top. Leave the cake to cool before removing it from the tin.

*TO STORE This cake keeps fresh for up to 2 weeks if covered and decorated with icing or wrapped in greaseproof paper and kept in an airtight container. Alternatively, wrap the cake in a double layer of greaseproof paper and aluminium foil and place in the freezer for up to 1 month. Allow to defrost overnight.

a

b

c

Mocha Coffee Cake

All-in-one • Coffee and chocolate have a strong affinity. Surely there is nothing more comforting than a hunk of chocolate cake with a freshly brewed mug of coffee? Here I have combined the two, using the simplest, one-stage, method to make the chocolate cake, then adding a velvety smooth coffee frosting.

1 Preheat the oven. Grease and line two 20cm (8in) round sandwich tins with non-stick baking paper, or use non-stick cake tins. Ensure all the ingredients are at room temperature. Put all the cake ingredients into a large clean bowl (a) and whisk with a handheld electric whisk for 8–10 minutes, until light and airy (b).

2 Divide the mixture between the prepared tins (c) and bake for 20–25 minutes, until the cake has shrunk away from the sides of the tin and is springy to the touch, and a skewer inserted into the middle of the cake comes out clean. Leave to cool in the tins for a few minutes before turning out onto a wire rack to cool completely.

3 Spread one cake with half of the coffee frosting and place the other cake on top. Spread the remaining frosting over the top cake and decorate with chocolate curls.

Variations
Variations can be made by replacing the cocoa with more flour, then adding:

• the seeds from 2 vanilla pods for a *vanilla cake*
• 2 tbsp ground cinnamon for a *spiced cake*
• the grated zest of 1 orange and 1 lemon for a *citrus cake*

For an alternative frosting, use vanilla cream cheese frosting (see p.56).

*TO STORE Once the frosting is on the cake, eat on the day.

For the cake:
• 200g (7oz) unsalted butter, plus extra for greasing
• 85g (3¼oz) cocoa powder
• 140g (5oz) self-raising flour
• 200g (7oz) golden caster sugar
• 4 eggs, lightly beaten
• 2 tbsp milk

For the filling and topping:
• 1 quantity coffee cream cheese frosting (see p.56)
• chocolate curls made using 50g (2oz) dark chocolate (see p.60)

• bake: fan 160°C (325°F)
• conventional 180°C (350°F) gas mark 4

Lemon and Poppy Seed Cake

All-in-one • This cake, with its combination of a zesty fresh lemon sponge and crunchy poppy seeds, is a winner. I have chosen to bake this cake in a classic kugelhopf tin, which is a great way to add visual interest to a plainer cake. The most appropriate topping for this cake is a lemon glacé icing – adding flavour, sweetness and moisture without detracting from the sharp flavour and interesting texture of the cake itself.

For the cake:
- 200g (7oz) unsalted butter, plus extra for greasing
- 225g (8oz) self-raising flour, plus extra for dusting
- 200g (7oz) golden caster sugar
- 4 large eggs
- 2 tbsp milk
- grated zest of 2 lemons
- 2 tbsp poppy seeds

For the topping:
- 1 quantity lemon glacé icing (see p.58)
- fresh edible flowers

- bake: fan 160°C (325°F)
- conventional 180°C (350°F) gas mark 4

1 Preheat the oven. Grease and flour the base and sides of a 15cm (6in) round kugelhopf tin. Ensure all the ingredients are at room temperature. Put all the ingredients into a large bowl and beat with an electric whisk for 8–10 minutes. Pour the mixture into the prepared tin.

2 Bake for 25–35 minutes until the cake has shrunk away from the sides of the tin and is springy to the touch. Leave to cool in the tin for a few minutes before turning out onto a wire rack to cool completely.

3 Cover with lemon glacé icing and decorate with fresh edible flowers.

*TO STORE Store for up to 5 days in an airtight container. Alternatively, wrap the cake in a double layer of greaseproof paper and aluminium foil and place in the freezer for up to 1 month.

Lime and Coconut Butterfly Buns

All-in-one • These deliciously fresh cakes combine the zest of fresh limes with creamed coconut. The quantity given here will make 24 butterfly cakes or one 20cm (8in) cake. A large cake works well covered with marzipan and sugar paste, and makes a great and unusual alternative for a birthday or christening cake.

For the cakes:
- 200g (7oz) unsalted butter
- 200g (7oz) golden caster sugar
- 200g (7oz) self-raising flour
- 4 eggs, lightly beaten
- 2 tbsp milk
- 100g (3¼oz) creamed coconut, grated

For the lime syrup:
- 50g (2oz) golden caster sugar
- 3 tbsp water
- grated zest and juice of 1 lime

For the topping:
- 1 quantity lime frosting (see p.57)
- 50g (2oz) toasted desiccated coconut or coconut flakes

- bake: fan 170°C (325°F)
- conventional 190°C (375°F) gas mark 5

1 Preheat the oven. Line 2 muffin trays with paper cases or place 24 silicone muffin cases on a baking sheet. Ensure all the ingredients are at room temperature. Put all the cake ingredients into a large bowl (a) and whisk together until you have a smooth mixture.

2 Spoon the mixture into the cases, filling to two-thirds full. Bake in the oven for 15–20 minutes until risen and light golden and the cakes spring back when pressed.

3 Meanwhile, place all the syrup ingredients in a saucepan and heat gently until dissolved. Brush each cake with the syrup as it comes out of the oven, then leave to cool on a wire rack.

4 Cut an inverted cone from the top of each cake by inserting a small sharp knife at an angle and cutting all the way round (b). Remove this cone, cut in half vertically (to make 'wings') and put to one side.

5 Fit a piping bag with a large star nozzle and fill with the lime frosting, then pipe it into the top of each cake until it is full.

6 Position the wings in the frosting (c). Sprinkle with toasted desiccated coconut or coconut flakes.

*TO STORE Store in an airtight container and eat within 2 days. Not suitable for freezing.

Cinnamon and White Chocolate Cupcakes

All-in-one • These cupcakes are deliciously moist, and the white chocolate buttercream makes them a decadent inclusion at any festive party. You could make even smaller, bitesized cupcakes and serve them at a chic canapé party, or present them in small boxes tied with ribbon.

For the cakes:
- 200g (7oz) unsalted butter
- 225g (8oz) self-raising flour
- 200g (7oz) golden caster sugar
- 4 eggs
- 2 tbsp milk
- 2 tbsp ground cinnamon

For the topping:
- 1 quantity white chocolate buttercream (see p.53)
- coloured sugar sprinkles

- bake: fan 160°C (325°F)
- conventional 180°C (350°F) gas mark 4

1 Line 2 muffin trays with paper cases or place 24 silicone muffin cases on a baking sheet. Ensure all the ingredients are at room temperature. Put all the cake ingredients into a large bowl and whisk with an electric whisk for 8–10 minutes.

2 Spoon the mixture into the cases, filling to two-thirds full (a). Bake in the oven for 15 minutes until risen and light golden and the cakes spring back when pressed. Remove from the oven and leave to cool on a wire rack, but still in the tin.

3 Spoon the white chocolate buttercream into a large piping bag fitted with a star nozzle and pipe swirls of buttercream on each cake. Decorate with the coloured sugar sprinkles.

*TO STORE Store in an airtight container and eat within 3 days. Not suitable for freezing.

a

Tropical Fruit Cake

All-in-one • For this lighter fruit cake, I have added some sunshine in the form of tropical fruits, including pineapple and mango. This cake is fruity and deliciously moist and nutty to eat. The addition of the chopped marzipan to the cake mixture gives a wonderful flavour and texture. I have chosen to finish the cake with a glazed fruit and nut topping, which makes this cake nutritious and easy to make. It is perfect for those who enjoy a good fruit cake without the need to further cover it with marzipan and icing – unless, of course, you are inspired to!

For the cake:
- 250g (9oz) unsalted butter, plus extra for greasing
- 140g (5oz) light brown sugar
- 6 large eggs, lightly beaten
- 85g (3¼oz) ground almonds
- 280g (10oz) plain flour
- 2 tsp ground ginger
- 2 tsp ground cinnamon
- 1 tsp baking powder
- 150g (5½oz) sultanas
- 100g (3½oz) raisins
- 200g (7oz) currants
- 100g (3½oz) naturally coloured glacé cherries
- 50g (2oz) dried mango, chopped
- 50g (2oz) dried pineapple, chopped
- 4 tbsp dark rum
- 140g (5oz) marzipan, cut into 1cm (½in) chunks

For the topping:
- 50g (2oz) hazelnuts, roughly chopped
- 50g (2oz) flaked almonds
- 85g (3¼oz) pecans, roughly chopped
- 150g (5½oz) apricot jam
- 150ml (5fl oz) brandy
- 40g (1½oz) dried apricots, roughly chopped
- 40g (1½oz) dried pineapple, roughly chopped
- 140g (5oz) naturally coloured glacé cherries, roughly chopped

- bake: fan 140°C (275°F)
- conventional 160°C (325°F) gas mark 3

1 Preheat the oven. Grease and line a deep 20cm (8in) square cake tin with non-stick baking paper or use a non-stick cake tin. Ensure all the ingredients are at room temperature. Place the butter, sugar, eggs and ground almonds in a bowl and sift in the flour, spices and baking powder. Beat with an electric whisk for 8–10 minutes until well mixed, light and fluffy. Fold in the dried fruits, rum and chopped marzipan (a).

2 Spoon the mixture into the prepared tin, level off the top with the back of a spoon, and bake for 1½ hours until a skewer inserted into the middle of the cake comes out clean. Remove the cake from the oven, but leave the oven on. Leave the cake to cool in the tin and turn out when cold.

3 While the cake is cooling, assemble the topping ingredients (b) and make the topping. Spread out the nuts on a baking tray and lightly toast in the oven until golden. Remove and leave to cool.

4 Place the apricot jam and brandy in a medium saucepan and bring gently to the boil, stirring continuously. Remove from the heat and stir in the fruit and toasted nuts until well blended.

5 Spread the topping over the fruit cake and leave for about 1 hour to set (c). The cake is now ready to be served (d).

*TO STORE Store for up to 2 weeks in an airtight container. Alternatively, wrap the cake in a double layer of greaseproof paper and aluminium foil and place in the freezer for up to 1 month.

TIP For the best result, use the semi-dried fruit available in the snack packs from most good supermarkets or independent food stores.

a b

c

d

Heavenly Orange and Strawberry Cake

Whisking • This fresh summery cake is light and airy but less moist than other cakes, as it contains so little butter. Similar in texture to a Swiss roll, this cake works well with lashings of fresh crème pâtissière and dressed with white chocolate-dipped strawberries. All you need for the perfect cake for the perfect summer's afternoon.

For the cake:
- 25g (1oz) unsalted butter, melted and cooled, plus extra for greasing
- 4 large eggs
- 100g (3½oz) golden caster sugar
- 50g (2oz) ground almonds
- grated zest of 1 orange
- 100g (3½oz) plain flour
- 1½ tsp baking powder

For the orange syrup:
- 50g (2oz) golden caster sugar
- 1 strip orange zest
- 2 tbsp Cointreau (optional)

For the filling and topping:
- ½ quantity crème pâtissière (see p.55)
- 225g (8oz) fresh strawberries, some sliced, some halved, some whole
- 8 chocolate-dipped strawberries (see p.60)

- bake: fan 140°C (275°F)
- conventional 160°C (325°F) gas mark 3

1 Preheat the oven. Grease and line a deep 20cm (8in) cake tin with non-stick baking paper or use a non-stick cake tin. Ensure all the ingredients are at room temperature. Whisk together the eggs and sugar with an electric whisk until the mixture thickens, turns pale and leaves a trail (a). This could take 8–10 minutes. Fold in the melted butter, ground almonds and orange zest (b) using a metal spoon. Sift the flour and baking powder into the mixture and fold into the mixture carefully (c).

2 Transfer the cake mixture to the prepared tin and bake for 30–40 minutes until firm to the touch and a skewer inserted into the middle of the cake comes out clean. Remove from the oven and leave to cool in the tin for 5 minutes before turning out on to a wire rack to cool.

3 To make the orange syrup, place the sugar, orange zest and 100ml (3½fl oz) water in a small saucepan and heat gently until dissolved, then boil hard for 2–3 minutes until syrupy. Leave to cool, then stir in the Cointreau, if using.

4 When ready to serve, split the cake in half and brush the cut surfaces with the syrup. Place the lower half of the cake on a plate or stand and pour over half the crème pâtissière, then cover with most of the sliced strawberries. Add the top half of the cake, pour over the remaining crème pâtissière and decorate with the remaining strawberries, including the chocolate-dipped ones.

*TO STORE Eat on the day of making, storing it in the fridge if necessary, but do not dress with the strawberries until ready to eat.

a

b

c

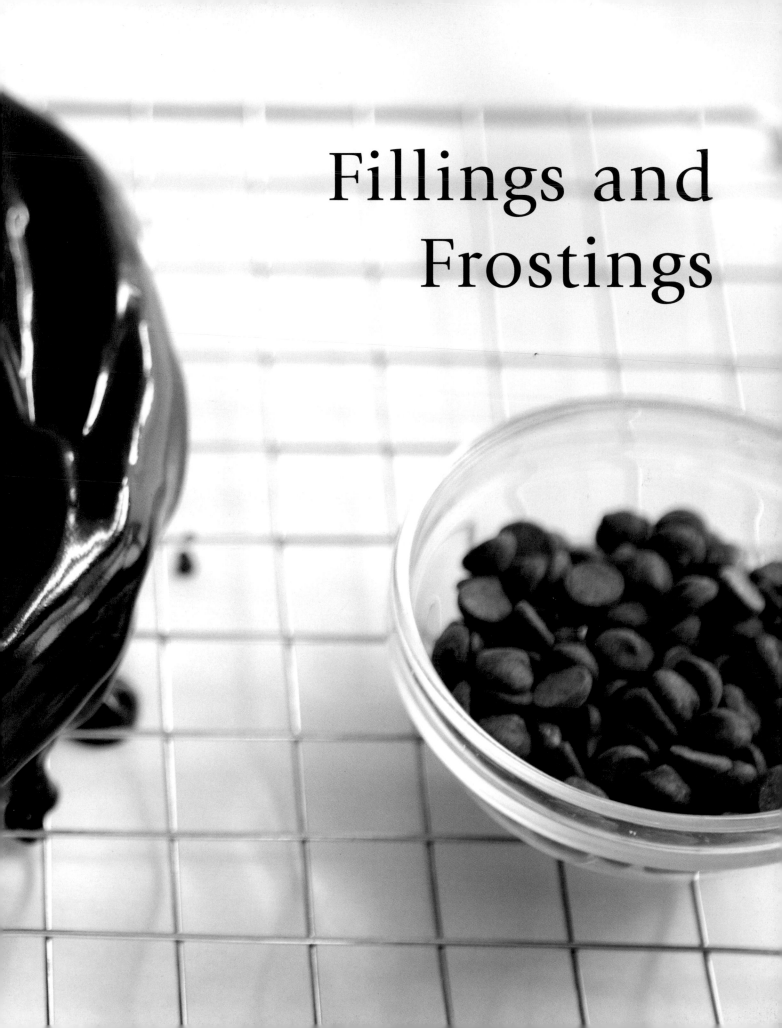

Fillings and Frostings

Once a cake is baked, it can be further embellished with a host of delicious fillings and frostings. Many of these can be interchanged on different cakes for different occasions. Frostings based on cream or cream cheese should be used only on cakes that can be refrigerated, and should be eaten within two days. Fresh fruit can safely be used as a filling or decoration with these cakes. Buttercreams are stable at ambient temperatures and are therefore perfect for any cakes that need to last a little longer or cannot be refrigerated. Avoid using fresh fruit with buttercream as a filling, as this will ferment at room temperature. Instead, opt for jam or lemon curd.

Chocolate Ganache

Chocolate ganache is the result of combining chocolate with cream to create a rich, velvet-smooth filling or frosting. Served warm, this can be poured over cakes for a wonderful frosting. Once chilled, it begins to thicken and can be used for piping pearls, beads or scrolls onto cakes (see opposite). It can also be combined with a basic vanilla buttercream (see p.52) to make a decadent filling for cakes.

You will need:
- 125ml (4fl oz) double cream
- 250g (9oz) unsalted butter, diced
- 500g (1lb 2oz) plain chocolate (70% cocoa solids), broken into pieces

- This makes enough to cover a 20cm (8in) cake with leftovers for piping.

1 Heat the double cream in a heavy saucepan until it begins to boil, then remove from the heat. Put the butter and chocolate in a bowl and place over a pan of simmering water to warm gently until just beginning to melt. Alternatively, melt in a microwave. Pour the cream over the chocolate and butter and stir gently to combine.

2 Beat the ganache with a wooden spoon until well combined, rich and glossy. Use straight away for pouring or allow to thicken for piping (see below). Alternatively, store in an airtight container in a refrigerator for up to 2 weeks or freeze for 3 months.

POURED GANACHE

1 Cover the top and sides of the cake with a thin layer of buttercream (see p.52) to seal the crumbs and edges and create a smooth base for the ganache. Chill the cake for 30 minutes in a fridge or 15 minutes in a freezer.

2 Place the cake on a wire rack over a sheet of silicone baking paper. Warm the ganache (if necessary) in a bowl over a pan of simmering water until glossy and smooth, then ladle it over the top and sides of the cake, using the base of the ladle or a palette knife to smooth it all over. Then, gently but firmly hold the wire rack and tap sharply onto the worktop to even out the ganache and ensure all areas of the cake are covered.

3 Use a palette knife to lift the cake gently from below to remove it from the rack and place it on a cake board or stand. Leave to set at room temperature, which may take 2–3 hours.

PIPED GANACHE

Ganache will thicken as it cools to room temperature. Beat well until it is firm enough to hold its shape, then spoon into a piping bag fitted with the appropriate icing nozzle. Note that if the ganache sets too firm in the piping bag or nozzle, you will need to empty the bag and gently reheat the ganache before filling a fresh bag.

TIP Warm the nozzle by running it under warm water and drying well before filling the piping bag with ganache. This will help to prevent the ganache setting in the nozzle and piping bag.

Buttercream

Any cake you intend to cover with marzipan, icing or chocolate plastique cannot be refrigerated. Therefore, these cakes cannot be layered with any filling that requires refrigeration. In such cases, buttercream is the perfect solution. This sweet frosting is perfectly stable at ambient temperature and can be flavoured or embellished to create the most delicious flavours to suit all palates and complement a wide range of cake flavours.

You will need:
- 175g (6oz) unsalted butter, softened
- 300g (10½oz) icing sugar, sifted
- seeds from 1 vanilla pod

1 Beat the butter in a mixing bowl with an electric whisk for 1 minute.

2 Add the icing sugar and beat slowly at first until blended, then on full speed until light and fluffy. Beat in the vanilla seeds (a).

Buttercream will keep for up to 2 weeks, stored in the fridge. You will need to bring it up to room temperature and beat again until light and fluffy before using.

Variations
Lemon Curd Buttercream
Add 175g (6oz) lemon curd to one quantity of the basic buttercream (above).

Rose Buttercream
3 tbsp rose syrup and a few drops of rose-pink concentrated edible food colouring into one quantity of the basic buttercream (above).

Orange Buttercream
Add the grated zest of 2 oranges to one quantity of the basic buttercream (above).

White Chocolate Buttercream

Break 100g (3½oz) white chocolate into a bowl and melt over simmering water or in a microwave. Cool, then beat into one quantity of the basic buttercream (opposite) until smooth and glossy (a). This will cover 24 cupcakes or fill and cover a 20cm (8in) cake.

Chocolate Ganache Buttercream

Make half a quantity of chocolate ganache (see p.51) and leave to cool, but not for so long that it sets. Add it to one quantity of the basic buttercream (opposite) and beat well. Chill to firm, then let the buttercream return to room temperature before beating well again. This can be stored in an airtight container in the frodge for up to 2 weeks. This will cover 24 cupcakes or fill and cover a 20cm (8in) cake.

Crème Pâtissière

You will need:
- 6 large egg yolks
- 1 tbsp vanilla extract
- 140g (5oz) caster sugar
- 50g (2oz) plain flour, sifted
- 600ml (20fl oz) milk
- 25g (1oz) butter, diced
- 142ml (4¾fl oz) carton double cream
- 500g (1lb 2oz) crème fraîche

Crème pâtissière is a deliciously fresh creamy custard that works very well with light cakes, especially if you want to turn them into a pudding. It will keep for up to 2 days in a refrigerator. Once served, it should be eaten within 4 hours.

1 Put the egg yolks, vanilla extract and caster sugar into a large mixing bowl. Whisk with an electric whisk until pale and thick.

2 Whisk in the flour until it is all incorporated.

3 Bring the milk to the boil in a heavy saucepan and gradually pour it into the egg mixture (decanting it first into a jug, if this is easier), whisking continuously.

4 Return the custard to the saucepan and cook over a gentle heat, stirring continuously, until thick and glossy. Continue to cook for 2 further minutes, stirring continuously, then remove from the heat and beat in the butter.

5 Pour the crème pâtissière into a clean bowl and cover with cling film, ensuring the film rests on the surface of the custard. Chill in the fridge. Whip the cream until firm (being careful not to over-whip it) and stir carefully into the cooled custard.

6 Stir in the crème fraîche just before serving. Use as a filling and/or topping.

*TO STORE Can be kept chilled at stage 5 for up to 2 days.

Cream Cheese Frostings

Cream cheese frostings have a strong affinity with cakes. The combination of full-fat cream cheese (ideally mascarpone) with sugar and additional flavours provides a variety of rich sweet frostings. More stable than fresh cream yet not as rich as buttercream, a cream cheese frosting is the perfect partner to many afternoon teatime cakes.

You will need:
- 2 x 250g (9oz) tubs mascarpone cheese
- 85g (3¼oz) golden caster sugar

Beat the mascarpone and sugar together until light and fluffy.

Variations
Orange Cream Cheese Frosting
Add the zest of 2 oranges and 5 drops of orange oil to 1 quantity of the basic recipe (above).

Vanilla Cream Cheese Frosting
Add the seeds of one vanilla pod or 1 tsp vanilla extract to 1 quantity of the basic recipe (above).

Coffee Cream Cheese Frosting
Beat the mascarpone and sugar together (a). Dissolve 3 tbsp instant coffee in 3 tbsp boiling water. Leave to cool, then add to 1 quantity of the basic recipe (above) (b). Whisk until combined (c). Use as desired (d).

a

b

c

d

Lime Frosting

Zesty lime and creamy coconut make the perfect frosting for filling or topping teatime cakes.

You will need:
- grated zest and juice of 2 limes
- 100g (3½oz) creamed coconut, grated
- 100g (3½oz) unsalted butter, softened
- 175g (6oz) icing sugar, sifted

1 Mix together the lime zest and juice and the creamed coconut. Microwave or place over a pan of simmering water until the coconut melts, then leave to cool.

2 Beat the butter until smooth and creamy using an electric whisk. Add the icing sugar and whisk slowly at first, then at full speed, until light and fluffy. Stir in the cooled coconut and lime mixture and whisk until light and mallowy.

Glacé Icing

This classic frosting combines icing sugar with water, which may be coloured and flavoured. Popular flavours are lemon, coffee and chocolate (see below). The icing should be mixed to a fairly runny consistency and is generally drizzled into position over large cakes, fairy cakes, tarts and buns, placed on a wire rack with a sheet of silicone baking paper underneath to catch the excess icing. Alternatively, it can be spooned over the top and sides of a cake. Leave to set for 15 minutes before transferring to a plate ready to decorate. It will set to the touch, but will not set firm like royal icing. As a result, it can be spooned into a piping bag and the end snipped to pipe very simple messages and line decoration, but cannot hold its shape, like royal icing, for more intricate piped decoration. The quantities listed here will be sufficient to decorate 24 cup/fairy cakes or cover one 15–20cm (6–8in) round larger cake. Once in place, the icing will last for up to 2 weeks (usually longer than the cake itself!). Any remaining glacé icing should be discarded.

Lemon Glacé Icing

You will need:
- juice of 2 lemons (strained to remove any pips and flesh pulp)
- 500g (1lb 2oz) icing sugar, sifted

1 Pour the lemon juice into a medium bowl and add the icing sugar a spoonful at a time, stirring well to remove any lumps.

2 Gently stir the sugar and juice together until you achieve a white icing that is no longer translucent but is still glossy and not dry or stiff. Spoon, pour or spread over cakes as required.

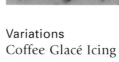

Variations
Coffee Glacé Icing
- 500g (1lb 2oz) icing sugar, sifted
- 2 tsp coffee granules dissolved in 4 tbsp boiling water

Follow the method for Lemon Glacé Icing (above), replacing the lemon juice with the coffee mixture.

Chocolate Glacé Icing
- 500g (1lb 2oz) icing sugar, sifted
- 1 tbsp cocoa powder dissolved in 4 tbsp boiling water

Follow the method for Lemon Glacé Icing (above), replacing the lemon juice with the cocoa mixture.

TIP Glacé icing adds lots of moisture, sweetness and flavour to cakes which makes it perfect for the all-in-one baked cakes. The technique is less complicated than some other toppings, so a great recipe for either beginners or children.

Chocolate Curls

These chocolate curls are a very simple standby for an effective decoration. They can be used to decorate large cakes, individual cakes or even ice cream. Use these decorations as soon as you have created them, as they tend to break up if stored.

1 Hold the bar of chocolate in one hand and the vegetable peeler in the other, then carefully but purposefully pull the peeler along the full length of the edge of the chocolate bar.

2 The chocolate curls will fall on to the worktop. Use a palette knife to gather them up carefully into a small bowl.

TIP The chocolate must be at room temperature for the peeler to run smoothly. If the chocolate is chilled or too cold, it will be brittle and the chocolate will not form nice curls.

You will need:
• bar of chocolate, at room temperature

Chocolate-dipped Strawberries

Chocolate-dipped strawberries are the epitome of luxury and decadence for a special occasion. Dipping strawberries in smooth white chocolate (or milk or dark, if you prefer) makes the perfect decoration for a summer party cake – either served as part of the decoration or accompanying the cake to dress the plate. The white chocolate will have to be tempered (a process of heating and cooling the chocolate to ensure it is pre-crystallized and sets with a shiny gloss finish and a clean 'snap' bite). This is done here using a much simpler method than usual, but one that achieves good results at home.

You will need:
• 200g (7oz) white chocolate drops
• 400g (14oz) (or about 20) strawberries, clean and dry but not chilled

1 Put half the chocolate drops in a heatproof bowl set over a saucepan of gently simmering water and leave until the chocolate melts. Remove the pan from the heat. (Alternatively, put the bowl in a microwave and heat on full power for 1 minute until melted.) Add the remaining chocolate drops to the melted chocolate a handful at a time and stir with a wooden spoon. This brings the temperature of the chocolate down – a vital part of the tempering process.

2 Stir with the wooden spoon until you feel the chocolate thicken slightly and move around the bowl with a definite 'clack', and until it coats the back of the wooden spoon with a glossy sheen that holds.

3 Hold each strawberry by the green calyx and dip into the white chocolate. Hold it there for a few seconds, then lift the strawberry out. Gently drag the strawberry on the side of the bowl to remove the excess chocolate.

4 Place it on a sheet of silicone baking paper to set at room temperature. Dip the remaining strawberries in the same way.

TIP The strawberries must be at room temperature, otherwise they will chill the white chocolate too quickly, which will affect the tempering. Chocolate-dipped must be eaten the same day, otherwise the shrink away from the chocolate. Do not refri chocolate-dipped fruit, as the chocolate will comes back up to room temperature with

2

3

4

Careful Covering
and Stacking

In this chapter I will show you how to cover a
variety of shapes and sizes of cakes with marzipan, sugar paste, chocolate plastique and royal icing. A flawless covering is fundamental to having the perfect canvas on which to decorate your cakes. Don't worry if your cakes are not perfect when starting out, as many undulations, bumps and bulges can be masked when you add the decoration later on. However, do practise on a dummy tier of polystyrene, if possible, as it can really help to build your confidence. Once your cakes are covered, I will show you how to dowel and stack them successfully so that they are secure, safe and even.

Note that cakes covered with marzipan and icing or chocolate plastique cannot be refrigerated once covered, as the icing or chocolate will pick up moisture in the fridge, which would adversely affect the texture.

TIPS Always wear a plain white cotton t-shirt when working, so that any fibres that land in the icing (you'd be surprised!) don't show up. Also, ensure you have all the equipment you need to hand, including a clean damp cloth, and sharpen your knife to give it a really clean edge. I like to work with a silicone rolling pin rather than a wood or marble one, as the former can impart a grain effect and the latter can affect the temperature of the covering.

Marzipan

The role of marzipan as a base coat is threefold:

- It gives the cake a really firm, smooth foundation on which to apply the top coat of sugar paste, chocolate plastique or royal icing.
- It is oil based (being made from almonds), which means it is perfect for locking in moisture, so helping to keep cakes moist.
- It will mask the colour of the cake bleeding through to the icing.

For a single-tier birthday cake, which may be served and eaten within 2–3 days of baking, it is not essential to cover it with marzipan first. I would, however, cover it with two thinner layers of sugar paste.

For a multi-tiered wedding cake, however, it is essential to have the initial layer of marzipan to ensure the cakes are firm and can support the dowels.

For fresher cakes (such as chocolate, vanilla and lemon), you could substitute the marzipan with a base coat of white chocolate plastique before adding the top coat.

Sugar paste

Sugar paste is a sweet icing rolled out like marzipan and used as the top coat for many celebration cakes and for lining boards. It is available commercially in a variety of colours, although white, ivory and chocolate are the most popular. Made from sugar, glucose syrup, water and a little vegetable oil, it covers beautifully and dries to a firm smooth finish with a soft sheen, and can easily be cut with a knife. It is the perfect canvas for further decoration, including hand piping, moulding and painting, as it is less porous than royal icing. It can be stored safely in a sealed polythene bag for up to 12 months and should be kneaded with minimal icing sugar until it is pliable and soft but not sticky.

BRUSHING WITH ALCOHOL
Cakes to be covered with sugar paste should have a base coat of marzipan, sugar paste or chocolate plastique, which should be brushed with brandy, or other alcohol, before the sugar paste top coat is applied. This reacts gently with the sugar in the base coat, forming a sticky glue for the sugar paste to adhere to. The alcohol acts as an antiseptic to help prevent mould growth between marzipan and sugar paste layers, which is of particular concern on a fruit cake, which

may be covered and decorated some considerable time before the celebration. This is less likely for a freshly baked sponge-based cake, as they are generally prepared within a week of the celebration and eaten soon after. There is little flavour added to the cake itself, so this is not a major concern for children's cakes. However, you can use cooled boiled water instead. Note that using boiled jam, as for attaching marzipan, is unsuitable here: it is too viscous and creates lumps.

Chocolate plastique

Chocolate plastique is malleable, yet sets firm and can be used to make hand-moulded roses, cut-out leaves and collars and fans for helterskelter-style cakes (see p.164). The roses, leaves and fans can be made up to 3 months in advance and stored in an airtight container at room temperature. They are perfect decorations for finishing individual cakes, adding to poured ganache chocolate cakes or adorning majestic wedding cakes.

Chocolate plastique on its own can be rather chewy, so it is best to mix it 1:1 with white or chocolate sugar paste when using it to cover cakes. White chocolate plastique (see p.74) is the perfect base coat for sponge-based cakes – such as vanilla, lemon or chocolate – as an alternative to marzipan. It creates a good base for a top coat of white or dark chocolate plastique (see p.75), or sugar paste. Follow the instructions for covering cakes with sugar paste.

Chocolate-covered and -decorated cakes tend to be less formal, less refined and more sculptural than iced cakes, with real wow factor. They can be easier to make, as many of the components are made ahead. However, cakes covered with a top coat of chocolate plastique will be more susceptible to temperature fluctuations. They will be very stable under the right conditions but will be badly affected by moisture, humidity and direct sunlight.

As a rule of thumb:

- Cakes should not be refrigerated: they are quite happy at room temperature.
- Cakes should not be allowed to get wet (avoid carrying these cakes to and from party venues in the rain, unless well covered).
- Cakes will droop if the humidity is high – which is of particular concern in marquees with no air conditioning.
- Cakes should not be placed in direct sunlight, as this will cause the chocolate to melt.

Covering individual cakes

All individual cakes smaller than 10cm (4in) should be cut out of one larger cake. This ensures that each cake is consistent in size and evenly baked and moist. I tend to bake 20cm (8in) square cakes, 7.5cm (3in) deep, which I cut in half horizontally, then cut out twenty-five 4cm (1½in) square cakes from each layer (so 50 in total), or sixteen 5cm (2in) round cakes (so 32 in total). If the cakes are to be filled, I cut the cake in half horizontally, as before, then split and fill each half with buttercream before cutting out the cakes. There will be less wastage from individual square cakes compared with round, though the trimmings from the latter can make the base of a delicious trifle. Individual cakes can be covered with marzipan and sugar paste, as I will show you here, but the method would be the same if you were covering with white or dark chocolate plastique (see p.74). Regardless of whether the top coat of chocolate is white, dark or combined, I would always recommend that the base coat be white chocolate plastique.

Covering individual square cakes

Cut each cake layer into 5 strips and then cut each strip into 5 squares, each measuring 4cm (1½in).

1 Knead the marzipan until smooth and pliable. This is a two-handed operation – one hand gently draws the outside to the centre while the other hand keeps the ball moving in a clockwise direction.

2 Dust the worktop liberally with icing sugar to prevent sticking. Use a rolling pin in short, sharp strokes in one direction only.

3 Lift the marzipan with a quarter turn and repeat rolling until it reaches the desired size and a thickness of 3mm (⅛in). Do not turn the marzipan over.

4 Use a pizza wheel to cut the marzipan into 10cm (4in) squares.

TIP The pizza wheel is a rotary cutter, and, as such, will not pull or snag the marzipan.

5 Brush each individual square cake with boiled, sieved apricot jam, using a pastry brush.

6 Lay one square of marzipan over the cake.

7 Let the marzipan fall down around the sides of the cake.

8 Shape the marzipan over the top and sides with your hands.

9 Use 2 straight-edged smoothers to press the marzipan onto the top and sides of the cake to create a neat cube shape.

10 Use a sharp knife to trim all the edges straight at the base of the cake. It is now ready to be iced.

Colouring sugar paste

1 To blend your own colour of sugar paste, use concentrated edible food colourings. Start with the required amount of white or ivory sugar paste and gently draw a cocktail stick dipped in one or a blend of colours across the sugar paste.

2 Wearing disposable latex or rubber gloves, gently knead the paste as described on p.66, building up the colour(s) until you reach the desired colour and intensity.

3 The only way to check if the colour is uniform throughout the entire piece of sugar paste is to cut it in half with a sharp knife. If there is any marbling effect, continue kneading until the colour is even.

Covering individual square cakes with sugar paste

1 Brush the top and sides of the marzipan-covered cake with brandy.

2 Roll out the sugar paste and cut into 10cm (4in) squares using a pizza wheel. Lay one square of sugar paste over the cake.

3 Shape the sugar paste over the top and sides with your hands.

4 Use 2 straight-edged smoothers to press the sugar paste onto the sides of the cake.

5 Press the sugar paste down on the top of the cake, too, to create a square shape.

6 Use a sharp knife to trim the edges straight at the base of the cake. It is now ready to be decorated.

Covering individual round cakes

Round cakes use 3 concentric circular cutters: 5cm (2in) for the cake, 6cm (2½in) for the marzipan base coat and 7cm (2¾in) for the sugar paste top coat.

1 Cut out the cakes with the 5cm (2in) cutter and brush with boiled, sieved apricot jam. If preferred, cut the cake layer into 4 strips first, then stamp out the cakes.

2 Roll out the marzipan and cut it into squares as for individual square cakes. Lay a square over a cake and shape to fit the top and sides with your hands. Use the 6cm (2½in) cutter over the top of the cake to trim and remove the excess marzipan.

TIP These individual cakes will handle better if they are chilled prior to being brushed with jam.

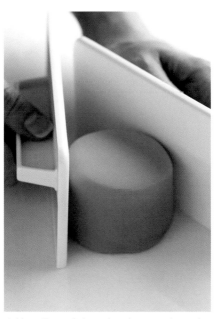

3 Brush with brandy and repeat with the sugar paste. Place the 7cm (2¾in) cutter over the top of the cake to remove the excess sugar paste.

4 Use 2 straight-edged smoothers in a gentle rotation motion to flatten, shape and smooth the cake. The cake is now ready for decoration.

Covering large cakes

Cakes that are going to be decorated should be covered with two layers: a base coat of marzipan, white chocolate plastique or sugar paste, and a flawless top coat of royal icing, sugar paste or chocolate plastique. If you want to top-coat the cake with royal icing, apply panels of marzipan, sugar paste or white chocolate plastique to the top and sides of a square cake separately (or a top panel and a large collar to go all around, for a round cake) to retain the sharp edges and give a crisp finish (see below). If you want to top-coat a round or square cake with any other covering, the base coat should be rolled out and laid over the cake in one sheet to give the cake a lovely rounded finish (see opposite).

Applying a base coat for a crisp, angular finish

1 Invert the cake on to a base board, usually 7.5cm (3in) larger than the cake, and ice in place in the centre of the board. Plug any gaps around the bottom with pieces of the base coat. Note: cakes that are to be royal iced sit on a large base board rather than a same-size cake board (see opposite).

2 Brush the top of the cake with boiled, sieved apricot jam. Roll out the base coat and cut a piece to fit the top of the cake. You can use a ruler, cake tin or cake board for this. Lift the base coat top into position and gently tease it out to fit right to the edges.

3 Use 2 straight-edged smoothers to neaten these edges so they are flush with the sides of the cake.

4 Brush the sides of the cake with more jam. Roll out more of the base coat and cut panels for the sides. Press one side in place.

5 Trim with a sharp knife as needed to achieve a flush finish, then add the remaining panels. (If you are covering a round cake, fix the large collar into position all round.)

Applying a base coat for a smooth, rounded finish

1 Knead the marzipan/sugar paste/white chocolate plastique until smooth and pliable, as described on p.66. Liberally dust the worktop with icing sugar and roll out the base coat to the desired size and thickness. Brush the cake (which, because it is not going to be royal iced, should already be on a cake board of the same size) with boiled, sieved apricot jam. Lift the base coat with both hands right underneath it so it rests over your hands, wrists and lower arms. Focus on the centre of the base coat and note the centre of the cake. Lift the base coat over the top of the cake and when the centre is directly over the centre of the cake, gently release the base coat from the centre outwards, removing your arms carefully to allow the base coat to fall into position over the cake. In this way, there is no stress applied to the base coat. It is not being pulled or forced over any edge of the cake or on a rolling pin and should have even length to cover all the sides.

2 Use your hands to cup the base coat over the sides of the cake to the base. For a square cake, tease the base coat over the corners of the cake first, gently skirting the base coat out to avoid any folds.

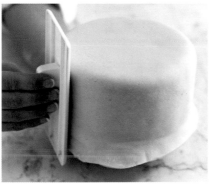

3 Use a straight-edged smoother to smooth the base coat over the top and sides of the cake to create a flat top and smooth sides.

4 Lift the cake on its board and continue to run around the sides with the smoother, encouraging the base coat down below the cake board. This will help you to create really straight sides and a perfect round base. Insert a sharp knife below the cake board, with the blade away from you, and cut the excess base coat away from the cake, pressing against and away from the cake board.

GUIDE TO QUANTITIES TO COVER CAKES WITH MARZIPAN/CHOCOLATE PLASTIQUE															● round cake ■ square cake
size of cake	10cm 4in ●	10cm 4in ■	15cm 6in ●	15cm 6in ■	20cm 8in ●	20cm 8in ■	23cm 9in ●	23cm 9in ■	25cm 10in ●	25cm 10in ■	30cm 12in ●	30cm 12in ■	35cm 14in ●	35cm 14in ■	40cm 16in ●	40cm 16in ■
quantity	400g 14oz	500g 1lb 2oz	600g 1lb 5oz	750g 1lb 10oz	800g 1lb 12oz	1kg 2lb 4oz	1kg 2lb 4oz	1.25kg 2lb 12oz	1.25kg 2lb 12oz	1.5kg 3lb 5oz	1.75kg 3lb 14oz	2kg 4lb 8oz	2.25kg 5lb	2.65kg 5lb 13oz	2.85kg 6lb 4oz	3kg 6lb 9 oz

Applying a sugar paste top coat on a round cake

1 Knead the sugar paste until smooth and pliable but not sticky. Brush the top and sides of the cake with brandy or cooled, boiled water (not the jam used for the base coat). Roll out the sugar paste on a worktop lightly dusted with icing sugar to the desired size and thickness, then drape it over the cake as described on p.71.

2 Use your hands to smooth and stick the icing over the top and sides of the cake.

3 Run over the top and sides of the cake with plastic smoothers (rounded for the top, straight-edged for the sides) until the sugar paste is completely smooth. Lift the cake on its cake board and use a sharp knife

at eye level to trim the excess sugar paste away from you against the cake board. The cake is now ready to be decorated.

TIP It can be easier to set the cake on a turntable to trim the excess sugar paste – as long as the turntable is smaller than the cake itself. Alternatively, use an upside-down bowl.

How to avoid sugar paste cracking

1 Make sure you knead it thoroughly so that it is warmed, malleable and pliable, but not sticky.
2 Add only a light dusting of icing sugar at the kneading stage to prevent it drying out.
3 Roll out no thinner than 4mm (1/6in) thick.
4 Add a second layer for a smoother finish and to avoid cracking over angular edges.
5 Handle the sugar paste lightly, lifting it gently and draping it over the top and sides of a cake, rather than stretching it.

GUIDE TO QUANTITIES TO COVER CAKES WITH SUGAR PASTE														● round cake ■ square cake
size of cake	15cm 6in ●	15cm 6in ■	20cm 8in ●	20cm 8in ■	23cm 9in ●	23cm 9in ■	25cm 10in ●	25cm 10in ■	30cm 12in ●	30cm 12in ■	35cm 14in ●	35cm 14in ■	40cm 16in ●	40cm 16in ■
quantity	750g 1lb 10oz	850g 1lb 14oz	1kg 2lb 4oz	1.25kg 2lb 12oz	1.25kg 2lb 12oz	1.5kg 3lb 5oz	1.5kg 3lb 5oz	1.8kg 4lb	2.1kg 4lb 12oz	2.35kg 5lb 3oz	2.7kg 6lb	3kg 6lb 9oz	3.25kg 7lb 2oz	3.5kg 7lb 11oz

GUIDE TO QUANTITIES TO COVER BASE BOARDS WITH SUGAR PASTE/CHOCOLATE PLASTIQUE															
size of board	18cm 7in ●	18cm 7in ■	20cm 8in ●	20cm 8in ■	23cm 9in ●	23cm 9in ■	25cm 10in ●	25cm 10in ■	28cm 11in ●	28cm 11in ■	30cm 12in ●	30cm 12in ■	33cm 13in ●	33cm 13in ■	35cm 14in ●	35cm 14in ■
quantity	315g 11oz	400g 14oz	420g 15oz	525g 1lb 3oz	550g 1lb 4oz	675g 1lb 8oz	650g 1lb 7oz	825g 1lb 13oz	800g 1lb 12oz	1kg 2lb 4oz	950g 2lb 2oz	1.2kg 2lb 11oz	1.2kg 2lb 11oz	1.4kg 3lb 2oz	1.3kg 3lb	1.6kg 3lb 8oz

size of board	38cm 15in ●	38cm 15in ■	40cm 16in ●	40cm 16in ■	45cm 18in ●	45cm 18in ■	50cm 20in ●	50cm 20in ■	55cm 22in ●	55cm 22in ■
quantity	1.5kg 3lb 5oz	1.9kg 4lb 3oz	1.7kg 3lb 12oz	2.1kg 4lb 12oz	2.2kg 4lb 14oz	2.7kg 6lb	2.6kg 5lb 12oz	3.3kg 7lb 4oz	3.2kg 7lb	4kg 9lb

Covering (lining) a base board with sugar paste

A cake looks professionally finished if the base board is also lined with sugar paste or chocolate plastique and edged in a double satin or grosgrain ribbon. Boards should be lined the day before the cakes are covered, to give them sufficient time to dry out overnight and make them easier to handle.

1 Brush the base board with water. Knead the sugar paste until smooth and pliable, then roll out on an icing sugar-dusted worktop to 3mm (⅛in) thick. Lift and place over the base board from the centre outwards. Use a straight-edged smoother to even and smooth the sugar paste over the base board.

2 Lift the board and use a sharp knife to trim the excess sugar paste by cutting against the board away from you. The edge of the base board should now be covered with some complementary ribbon of the correct width, fixed in place with a little glue.

3 Once the cake is covered, spread a little royal icing in the centre of the board to hold it.

4 Use 2 hands to hold the cake from underneath and gently set the cake down into position on the base board. Use 2 plastic straight-edged smoothers to nudge the cake so it is centrally positioned and smoothed against the base board. The cake is now ready to be decorated.

TIP Ensure your knife is really sharp, and clean it between each trim for a really clean, professional finish. Leave the cake to dry overnight.

Making glitter boards

For added glamour and a sense of occasion, it can be fun to cover base boards with a different-coloured sugar paste and add edible glitter. This is a great way to create the impression of a larger cake and to incorporate glitter that won't actually be eaten.

1 Cover the board as described above, using the coloured sugar paste of your choice. Lay the board on a large sheet of silicone baking paper. Spray the covered board with edible varnish or brush with sugar glue.

2 Liberally dredge the base board with edible glitter in a complementary colour. Wait for a few moments before shaking off the excess. Leave to firm overnight.

Chocolate Plastique

Chocolate plastique is a soft, pliable paste made from chocolate, glucose syrup and stock syrup. It can be rolled out like marzipan but has all the taste of chocolate. It can be bought from specialist cake-decorating stores or made at home.

Plastique Stock Syrup

You will need:
- 140g (5oz) caster sugar
- 85ml (3¼ fl oz) glucose syrup

- Yields 450ml (16 fl oz)

Place the sugar, glucose syrup and 250ml (9fl oz) water (a) in a saucepan and bring to the boil. Remove from the heat and leave to cool.

This recipe will provide slightly more than is required for the white chocolate plastique recipe here.

TIP Make chocolate plastique in large batches, as it will keep happily at room temperature for up to 3 months. Begin preparing the plastique at least 1 week before you need it, as it can take some time to set. For milk chocolate plastique, mix equal quantities of white and dark together.

White Chocolate Plastique

You will need:
- 1.75kg (3lb 12oz) white chocolate buttons
- 115g (4oz) cocoa butter buttons
- 400ml (14 fl oz) glucose syrup
- 300ml (10fl oz) plastique stock syrup (left)

- Yields 2.5kg (5lb 8oz)

1 Melt the chocolate buttons in a microwave or in a large heat-proof bowl placed over a pan of simmering water. Melt the cocoa butter buttons in a separate bowl. Once they have both melted, mix them together and stir well. (Their different melting points mean that they need to be melted separately. Both need to be melted completely, but not overheated, for this recipe to work.)

2 Measure the glucose syrup and stock syrup together in a clean bowl and warm in the microwave. (This brings the temperature up to similar to that of the white chocolate.)

3 Pour the chocolate mixture over the glucose and stock syrup (b) and mix with a wooden spoon until smooth. It should cling to the spoon and leave the sides of the bowl clean (c).

4 Transfer into a large freezer bag and spread the paste out so that as much surface area touches the bag as possible. This will speed up the setting process. Leave overnight and then for up to 3 days to set firm. The chocolate plastique can now be stored at room temperature for up to 3 months, if required.

5 When ready to use, turn the bag inside out and peel it away from the plastique. Knead until smooth and pliable. If the paste is really soft, due to a warm room, add plenty of icing sugar until it thickens and is smooth. If it is really firm, due to a cold room, microwave it for 10 seconds at a time until it softens and is malleable.

a

b

c

Dark Chocolate Plastique

You will need:

- 1.25kg (2lb 12oz) plain chocolate buttons (maximum 55% cocoa solids)
- 700g (1lb 9oz) glucose syrup
- Yields 1.8kg (4lb)

1 Melt the chocolate in a microwave or in a large heat-resistant bowl placed over a pan of simmering water. Leave to cool slightly.

2 Heat the glucose syrup in a pan or a microwave so it is at a similar temperature to the chocolate. Pour into a large bowl (a).

3 Gradually beat the chocolate into the glucose syrup, beating it to a thick paste that leaves the sides of the bowl clean (b). Transfer to a large freezer bag and leave overnight to set. Store at room temperature for up to 3 months.

4 When ready to use, turn the bag inside out and peel away from the plastique. Knead until smooth and pliable. If the paste is really firm, microwave for 10 seconds at a time until it softens and is malleable.

TIP Using plain chocolate with maximum 55% cocoa solids prevents the paste from splitting and being too bitter.

a

b

Royal Icing

Royal icing combines fresh egg white with icing sugar and a little lemon juice to create a rich, thick, glossy icing that can be used to cover cakes, add additional elaborate piping or be used for run-outs. The albumen (protein) in egg white gives the icing its elasticity and viscosity, and enables it to set firm once dried. The lemon juice strengthens the egg white and gives the icing a pleasant taste. Once a batch of royal icing has been made, it can be stored safely in a sealed airtight container for up to 7 days if kept cool and dry. Beat the icing well each time before use. The standard recipe, which is ideal for piping, can have glycerine added to it to give a softer set, making it ideal for covering. Alternatively, it can have water added to make a flooding icing (see p.79).

You will need:
- 1 large egg white, at room temperature
- 450g (1lb) (approx.) icing sugar, sifted
- ½ lemon, cut into wedges

1 Assemble the ingredients.

2 Put the egg white in a large and very clean bowl.

3 Whisk on full speed until it reaches the soft peak stage.

4 Add two-thirds of the icing sugar and whisk slowly at first, then on full speed for 2 minutes.

5 Continue to add the icing sugar until the icing resembles freshly whipped double cream. It should have a firm peak but still be glossy – not grainy or powdery. It should be mallowy, like meringue. (You may not need all the sugar.)

6 Squeeze the lemon wedges through a tea strainer (to remove any pips and the fleshy pulp) into the icing. Whisk for a further minute. The icing is now ready to use for piping.

Royal Icing for Covering

Add 1 tsp glycerine to the icing and whisk for a further minute. The glycerine allows the royal icing to retain some softness as it sets once it has been spread over the cake. This makes it smoother and less brittle, and easier to cut. Do not attempt to use this icing for piping, as it has a tendency to crumble.

You will need these quantities:
- For a 15cm (6in) cake: 2 quantities
- For a 20cm (8in) cake: 2½ quantities
- For a 25cm (10in) cake: 3 quantities
- For a 30cm (12in) cake: 4 quantities

Colouring royal icing

1 Use a cocktail stick and concentrated edible food colour to add colour to royal icing of the desired consistency. Add sparingly to build up the desired intensity.

2 Use a metal spoon to avoid adding air bubbles, and stir thoroughly to make sure the colour is dispersed evenly throughout the icing.

Flooding icing

TIP Always store royal icing in a
sealed airtight container or in a bowl
covered with a clean damp cloth to
prevent it from crusting over.

Royal icing can be thinned down and used to create run-outs (see p.97).
These can be applied directly onto the top of a cake or piped separately onto
silicone baking paper and left to dry before being applied to cakes.

Flooding icing can be thinned down using either water (a) or egg white.
Water will allow the run-out to dry quickly, but the icing will be less strong
and so is more suitable for smaller run-outs like butterflies and flowers. Egg
white will create a stronger run-out but will take longer to dry and is more
suitable for larger run-outs.

Add the liquid drop by drop to fresh royal icing (with no glycerine added) and
stir with a metal spoon until the icing leaves a trail that, by the count of 10,
has disappeared into the bowl of icing (b).

Flooding icing should be used in a piping bag with no nozzle. Snip the end of
the bag just before use and squeeze into a second bag to remove any air
bubbles. Snip the end of this bag and use the icing immediately.

a

b

Applying a royal icing top coat

I devised this method for covering cakes with royal icing to deal with a number of modern-day issues – how to royal ice a sponge cake for it to remain fresh for a celebration; and how to have the appearance and taste of royal icing with the ease of cutting of sugar paste. Here is the solution. The cake is first covered with panels of sugar paste, and just one final top coat of royal icing is applied to seal the cake and give the all-important royal-iced finish. This method is much less time consuming than building up a number of layers of royal icing to achieve the desired thickness, so it can be used for fresh sponge cakes baked and iced much closer to the celebration. This technique also ensures the cake will still cut beautifully, as there is only one thin coat of royal icing over a sugar paste base. A thicker layer of royal icing tends to be hard and brittle.

1 Follow the process on p.70, using panels of sugar paste instead of marzipan. (If you are using a round cake, cut one large collar and fix into position all round the sides.)

2 Make a batch of fresh royal icing with glycerine (see p.77). Starting on the top, use a palette knife to spread sufficient icing over the cake, using a paddling motion to smooth and remove excess air bubbles.

3 Hold an icing ruler at a 45-degree angle and, slowly but smoothly, draw the ruler towards you to create a smooth final top coat of icing. This process can be repeated a number of times until you are happy with the finish. Trim the edges with a sharp knife. Leave to set for at least 4 hours or overnight.

4 For a square cake, spread the icing over two opposite sides first. Then, using a royal-ice metal scraper and holding it at a 45-degree angle in contact with the base board, draw the scraper smoothly towards you. Repeat on the other two sides.

For a round cake, place it on a turntable. Hold the scraper against the side of the cake and, with the other hand, turn the turntable one full circle (revolution) in a smooth motion. This will give a clean finish all the way around the cake.

5 Trim the top and sides with a sharp knife, and leave to set for 4 hours or overnight. Finally, use a palette knife to apply royal icing to the base board and use the scraper to smooth all the way around. Use a sharp knife to trim away the excess against the base board. (Again, a round cake can have the board covered on a turntable for ease.) Leave to set for at least 4 hours or overnight. The iced cake is now ready to be decorated.

Stacking

Whichever method of stacking you choose, make sure that you use only those cakes that are firm and have set properly; that all tiers are placed on thick cake boards first; and that the plastic dowelling rods (which are removed when the cake is cut) are cut and trimmed evenly. Use more rods for softer or heavier cakes to provide maximum support. To dowel and stack a number of tiers, dowel each tier separately first before assembling the entire cake when instructed, fixing the tiers into position with royal icing. Check from all sides that the cake is evenly placed on the tier below. Leave each tier to set for 15 minutes before proceeding with the next tier. Finally, use a spirit level to ensure the base table and tiers are even as you assemble a cake (especially useful if setting up a cake in a marquee).

1

2

3

4

Blocking

You will need:

- 5cm (2in) or 7.5cm (3in) deep polystyrene block, round or square, depending on the shape of the tiers, 10cm (4in) smaller than the dimension of the lower tier
- 4 dowelling rods per tier for cakes up to and including 25cm (10in) in diameter, and 8 rods per tier for cakes larger than that
- marker pen
- ruler
- sharp, heavy-duty scissors
- spirit level

Blocking is the name for tiers that have been stacked with a polystyrene block between them to be filled with sugar or fresh flowers. This is a more contemporary style than traditional pillars, and creates additional height, as well as contributing to the overall design. I recommend a 5cm (2in) gap between tiers for a single row of flowers and 7.5cm (3in) for a double row. With this technique, it is essential to cut each dowelling rod to the height of the polystyrene block used between the tiers (plus the height of the cake below). The block adds surface area and a medium into which to insert fresh wired or sugar flowers and ribbons. The rods support the tiers and hold the polystyrene block securely in position, which means it does not need to be iced into position.

1 Place the base tier on a level worktop and position the polystyrene block in the centre of the cake. Hold the block with one hand and gently but firmly insert the dowelling rods evenly spaced around the outside up against the block. Push them all the way to the base of the cake until they reach the base board.

2 Use a marker pen to mark on the inside of each dowel where it is level with the polystyrene block.

3 Remove all the dowels carefully. Lay them down and line them up against a level edge, and mark one clear line using the marker pen and the ruler across the average height. This will level the surface for the next tier if this tier is uneven. Cut each dowelling rod with heavy-duty scissors at the marked line, then hold them all together on a flat surface to check they are all even. Trim if necessary. Reinsert all the dowelling rods.

4 Place the next tier into position. The tier should be stable and firm and not wobble. If it does wobble, remove all the dowelling rods, trim each by 2mm (⅛in), check they are all even, then reinsert. The upper tier should now sit firmly in position. Repeat for further tiers.

Direct stacking

You will need:
- 6 dowelling rods per tier
- ruler
- marker pen
- sharp, heavy-duty scissors
- spirit level

Stacking tiers directly on top of one another is the safest method to stack cakes and creates the illusion of one large cake. This is the perfect solution for cakes that have to be transported some distance.

1 Place the base tier on a level worktop and insert the first dowelling rod in the centre of the cake, pushing it down until it reaches the base board. Use a pen to mark the dowel in line with the top of the cake. Remove the dowel carefully. Lay and line up this dowel with 5 others so the mark is clearly visible. Place a ruler across the dowels at the mark and use a marker pen to mark the other 5 dowels at the same

position. Cut each dowelling rod with heavy-duty scissors at the marked line, then hold them all together on a flat surface to check they are all even. Trim if necessary.

2 Insert the dowels into the cake, making sure they remain within the base area of the next tier (offset, if relevant). Push them all the way down until they reach the board.

3 Spread a small amount of royal icing onto the surface of the cake over the rods to fix the next tier into position.

4 Place the upper tier in position.

Stacking with a central column

You will need:
- ribbon for polystyrene block, 25mm (1in) wide
- glue stick
- 6 dowelling rods per tier
- 2.5cm (1in) deep polystyrene block, round or square, depending on the shape of the tiers, 10cm (4in) smaller than the dimension of the base tier
- ruler
- marker pen
- sharp, heavy-duty scissors
- spirit level

Central columns made from polystyrene add additional height to a tiered cake. Wrap in a complementing ribbon, fixed with glue. They are clearly visible, so the dowelling rods have to be concealed beneath the polystyrene block. This method is less stable than stacking or blocking, so should be recommended only on smaller cakes and never in a marquee, where a stable floor cannot be guaranteed!

Follow steps 1–2 of the direct stacking method, making sure the dowels remain

within the base area of the polystyrene block to go on top.

3 Spread a small amount of royal icing onto the surface of the cake over the dowelling rods and fix the central column into position.

4 Check that the column is central and even with a spirit level. Leave to set for 15 minutes, then place the next tier on top. Repeat for more tiers, as necessary, letting each column set in between.

Masterclass

In this chapter I am going to show you the tricks of my trade. These will enable you to build up your own repertoire of intricate decorations that can be applied to so many cake designs. The masterclass will include hand piping, hand moulding, hand painting, cutters and ribbons. Many of these techniques are relatively simple, yet effective to achieve, making them relevant to a commercial market and the time-strapped cake decorator. Beautiful wired flowers can look stunning, but they are painstaking and lengthy to make. I have therefore made a conscious decision not to include these in this book, focusing more on a larger number of less time-consuming techniques. You will find cakes featuring all these general techniques in the Cake Gallery (pp.116–211).

Hand piping

Hand piping is an instant and gratifying technique used to decorate cakes. From creating a simple hand-piped message to more elaborate basket-weaving or pressure-piped scrolls, the skill lies in holding the piping bag correctly, working with the right consistency of royal icing and having the confidence to work directly onto the cake. In many of my masterclasses, I find students need a little encouragement and practice to build up their confidence. I therefore encourage them (and you) to practise these techniques on a plain iced board or an iced dummy cake. It is important to feel the viscosity of the icing, to know how much pressure to apply and the correct speed at which to move the piping bag. To allow the icing to flow smoothly, always pull the piping bag in the same direction as the flow of icing.

Making a piping bag

It is a good idea to get into the habit of making your own piping bags from silicone paper. These are less expensive than ready-bought disposable piping bags and more hygienic than reusable piping bags.

1 Take a large sheet of silicone paper and divide it into equilateral triangles by folding and trimming with a small sharp knife, to use the entire sheet of paper. You can make piping bags of different sizes, which will be useful for different piping tasks. Start with one triangle in front of you – long side away from you and the opposite point facing you.

2 Bring the back of the left-hand point of the triangle down to meet the centre point.

3 Lift the piping bag up, holding the 2 points that now meet in the centre. Bring the right-hand point over the front of the bag all the way round to the back to meet the 2 points, so they all line up together.

4 Gently tease the base of the piping bag until the points line up and the bag is nice and taut and forms a sharp point at the tip of the bag.

5 Fold the base of the piping bag over on itself to seal, or staple twice.

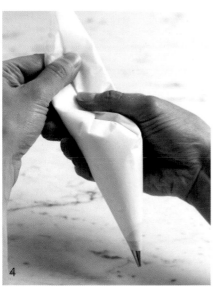

Hand piping

1 Cut about 2cm (¾in) off the point of a piping bag.

2 Drop an icing nozzle into the bag. Hold the bag in your hand like a cone, with the join facing away from you. Spoon the royal icing into the bag as shown – no more than half full.

3 Press the front of the bag down so it is flush with the icing (this will begin to expel the air from the bag).

4 Fold the left-hand side of the bag inwards, followed by the right-hand side, as shown.

5 Finally, fold and roll the top of the bag downwards until it is secure. The piping bag is now ready to use.

6 Hand piping is a 2-handed operation. Hold the piping bag in the hand you write with, between your first and second fingers. Use your thumb as the pressure pad on the back of the bag. Your thumb will apply all the pressure to force the icing out; the fingers merely hold the bag and direct the nozzle. Place the first finger of your other hand near the base of the nozzle to control its direction.

If you are piping on the sides of the cake, rest the base of both hands on the edge of the turntable, worktop or (very lightly) the cake below. If you are piping on the top of the cake, rest the hand that is not holding the bag on the base, turntable or worktop and have the piping hand rest on top of this one, so that at least one hand is in contact with a stable surface to steady the piping hand.

Make contact at the start and end of the piping, but lift the nozzle away from the cake and let the icing fall into position on the cake in between.

Hand-piped pearls and lines

Pearls are the most simple technique, yet they need to be executed cleanly to look professional and uniform. Pearls can be piped in a number of sizes, ranging from a delicate size no. 1 icing nozzle through 1.5, 2 and 3, to large pea-sized no. 4 pearls. The smaller the pearl, the easier it will be to disguise the peak that will inevitably form as you withdraw the nozzle. For larger pearls, this is harder to disguise, as the aperture is naturally that much larger, and peaks should be carefully dampened down with a moist paintbrush.

For perfect pearls, whether on the top, side or base of the cake, hold the piping bag perpendicular to the cake and just a smidgen away from it. As you apply pressure, the icing comes into contact with the cake to create a perfect round base. Continue to apply pressure to allow the icing to build up to the desired size, then release the pressure and gently snatch the nozzle away at the same time and at the same angle to leave a perfect pearl (a).

Hand-piped lines
These nozzles can also be used to pipe vertical lines, from very fine (see Candy stripes, opposite) to chunky (b).

Line loops
Line loops are easily achieved with plain nozzles. Make contact at the start of the loop and again at the end, but pull the piping bag away from the cake as the loop is formed, to maintain a smooth loop (c).

Pearl loops
To build up confidence or additional texture, loops can be created by piping a trail of pearls that tail off before piping the next pearl, so they join up (d).

a

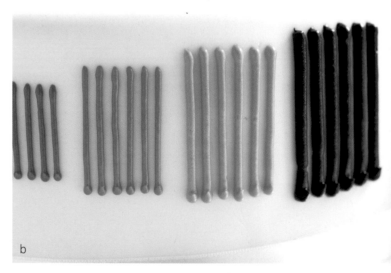

b

c

d

Candy stripes

Candy-striping cakes is a skilful technique that requires a steady hand and practice. It is effective for both individual and larger round cakes. Working with 3 colours of royal icing, this can be one of the most effective techniques to create a more masculine cake.

Add a few drops of water to the icing so that it is slightly slacker than usual, as this helps the icing to flow smoothly without breaking, helps the icing to adhere well to the cake and reduces air bubbles. Fill three piping bags, each fitted with a no. 3 plain nozzle, with three different colours of icing, and seal the bags.

Place the piping bags in a sealable freezer bag and use one at a time to prevent the royal icing drying out in the bags.

For individual cakes, place the cakes on silver or gold cake cards prior to piping, so they can be handled once they have been decorated. Start the icing lines at the top of the cakes, as shown, and bring them right down to the base.

For large cakes, place an upturned cake board the same size as the cake on top of a covered cake and draw around the outside with a pokey tool. This will mark the top edge of the cake and be the guide from which you will always pipe down. This can be more time-consuming than the method for small cakes, but it is the only way to achieve accurate spacing.

TIP Remember to pinch the end of the nozzle each time you pick up a piping bag to ensure clean contact is made with the cake.

1 Place a cake in the centre of a turntable and start with the white icing (if using), or else the palest colour, and pipe a vertical line from the top edge to the base of the cake. Make contact at the top of the cake, then gently life the icing away from the cake as you move the piping bag downwards. The icing should be coming out of the icing nozzle at right angles to the cake. Make contact at the base of the cake and allow the nozzle to build up a small pearl of royal icing before releasing the pressure and removing the nozzle. Repeat this around the cake 12 times to resemble a clock face, to set the spacing.

2 With the second colour, pipe a vertical line parallel to the first colour, ensuring you leave sufficient space for the third colour. The lines should be parallel but not touching each other.

3 Apply the third colour of candy stripes around the cake. Leave to set.

Scrolls and stars

Using a star icing nozzle, you can create single stars, textured piped lines and scrolls. For single stars, hold the star nozzle at right angles to the cake and pipe as though for a pearl to create a star (a). To pipe a star trail – a trail of star pearls around the base of a cake (b) – use a no. 5 star nozzle.

1 For star scrolls, hold the icing nozzle against the top edge of the cake and begin to pipe to build up a star pearl, pulling the piping bag below the pearl and to the right to tail off against the cake.

2 Pipe the next star scroll over the top of the end of the tail and bring the tail out of the top of the pearl towards the right, so creating a wave effect.

3 Continue working along the top of the cake in this manner until you finish the line of star scrolls.

Hand-piped bows

I pipe delicate bows using a no. 1.5 or no. 2 nozzle. Start in the centre of the bow and pipe a triangle out to the top left, down to the bottom left, then back to the centre. Touch the piping bag against the cake at these 3 points. Then move the piping bag out to the top right, down to the bottom right, then back to the centre (a). Finish by piping the 2 tails from the centre downwards (b).

Hand-piped leaves

I just love the expression on the face of anyone who sees these royal iced leaves being piped without an icing nozzle or, indeed, has a go themselves. The royal icing is spooned into a piping bag with no nozzle. The technique relies on the decorator snipping the end of the piping bag evenly, and then pressure-piping (see p.94) to achieve these perfect leaves. The larger the snip, the bigger the leaf; the smaller the snip, the more delicate the leaf. What I particularly like is the fact that every leaf will be slightly different, making them so interesting. You could also use this technique with chocolate ganache.

Practise these leaves on a clean work surface or sheet of silicone paper until mastered; the icing can then be scraped up and spooned into a fresh piping bag. Alternatively, keep the ones you like and once they have dried overnight, peel them off with a small palette knife and ice them into position on your cake.

The most common areas people struggle with are not allowing the icing to build up before wiggling and moving the bag towards them, moving the bag too fast and not releasing the pressure before pulling the leaf to a point.

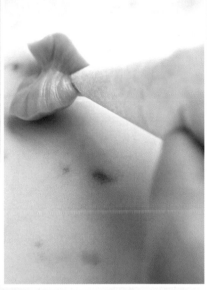

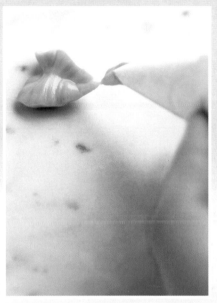

1 Fill a piping bag with green royal icing (add a little icing sugar to ensure it is on the stiffer side) and seal the bag. Use a sharp pair of scissors to snip across the end of the piping bag at an angle, as shown and repeat the other way to create a V.

2 Hold the piping bag so the tip is flat, with the slits of the V to the sides, in contact with the cake. Apply pressure to the piping bag so the icing begins to build up. Gently lift the piping bag just off the cake and wiggle the bag gently from side to side using small smooth movements of your wrist, as you now gently pull the piping bag towards you.

3 Release the pressure on the bag then pull the bag towards you and slightly upwards to finish the leaf with a long tongue with a nice point.

Pressure piping

Our Little Venice lace design is hand piped using pressure piping. This is where the icing is built up on the cake and remains in contact with the cake rather than the nozzle being lifted and allowing the icing to fall into position. Depending on the design to be piped, I suggest a no. 2 or 3 nozzle is best to work with. The royal icing should be stiff but still glossy.

You will need:
• royal icing

Equipment:
• tracing paper and fine-liner pen
• pokey tool
• piping bag
• no. 2 icing nozzle

1 Trace the template on p.216, spacing the designs regularly around the cake. Fix the tracing paper to the cake and prick through the design with a pokey tool. Mark the centre of all the pearls or beginning points of the scrolls with the pokey tool. Fit a piping bag with a no. 2 nozzle and fill with icing.

2 Pipe the 2 outer scrolls, bringing each inwards and downwards.

3 Pipe the highest 2 scrolls, which should come between the second-highest scroll and the pearl above.

4 Pipe the second line of scrolls up to and just on the first scroll line.

5 Pipe the third scrolls down; these are a little thicker, which is achieved by applying a little more pressure.

6 Pipe the first 2 vertical scrolls.

7 Pipe the smaller 2 vertical scrolls beneath the first.

8 Pipe the 2 outer pearls along the top edge.

9 Pipe the 2 base pearls of the top, which are slightly more elongated.

10 Pipe 2 rounder pearls above and finish with one elongated pearl at the very top of the design.

TIPS Start symmetrical designs at the top and work downwards. Bring the left and right scrolls together to the centre line. First pipe the left- and then immediately the right-hand mirror image of each separate scroll before moving on to the next mirrored pair.

Basket weave

This technique never fails to impress. Two piping bags are used: one to create the vertical straight line and the other for the horizontal woven effect. The skill is keeping all the lines even and straight.

1 Place an upturned cake board the same size as the cake on top of a covered cake and draw around the outside with a pokey tool. This will mark the top edge of the cake and be the guide from which you will always pipe down.

2 Fill 2 piping bags – one fitted with a no. 3 plain nozzle, the other with a no. 19B basket-weave grooved nozzle – with white royal icing, and seal the bags. Starting with the plain nozzle, pipe a vertical line from the top edge to the base.

3 Now change to the basket-weave nozzle and hold it flat against the cake to the left of the piped line. Make contact with the cake as you begin to pipe, lifting the bag slightly away from the cake to create a gentle wave back on itself, and then bring the nozzle across the line horizontally and straight, tailing the icing away. The basket piping should be approximately 1.5cm (⅝in) long.

4 Leave a gap the same width as the basket piping, then repeat the piping directly below the first line, and then all the way to the base of the cake – always leaving a gap (a).

5 Pipe the next vertical line approximately 1cm (⅜in) away from, and parallel to, the first line, covering the tails of the basket piping (b).

6 Pipe the first row of the next section of basket piping between the first and second rows of the first section, so the icing starts at the first vertical line, pipes over the second vertical line, then tails away.

7 Repeat this technique all the way around the cake, keeping the pressure even all the way around, so the basket weave doesn't end up with gaps or is uneven.

TIPS Don't underestimate how much royal icing you will require for the basket piping – you will need several bags to decorate one tier.

Always start at the back of the cake in case the piping doesn't line up when you get all the way around. The front of the cake can then be positioned on show.

You will need:
- white royal icing

Equipment:
- cake board
- pokey tool
- 2 piping bags
- no. 3 icing nozzle
- no. 19B basket-weave grooved icing nozzle

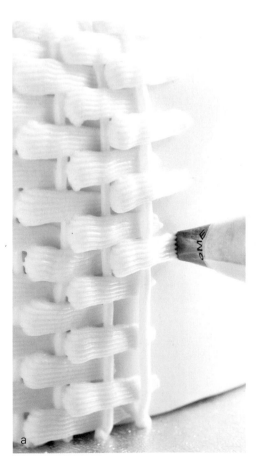

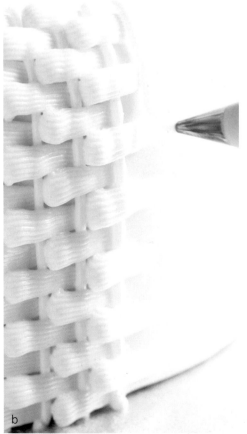

Run-outs

Piped outlines can be filled with icing to create effective decorations, such as the butterflies shown here. Diluting the icing to flooding consistency enables it to run out into the areas within the iced lines.

You will need:
• royal icing in 2 colours: white for the outlines and bodies and a coloured flooding icing (see p.79) for the wings

Equipment:
• tracing paper and fine-liner pen
• cake board
• masking tape
• waxed paper
• piping bags
• no. 1.5 icing nozzle
• paintbrush

1 To make the butterflies, trace the template on p.214 enough times for all the butterflies you want, and fix the tracing paper onto a cake board with masking tape. Fix a sheet of waxed paper over the top with masking tape. Fit a piping bag with the icing nozzle and fill with some of the white royal icing. Pipe the outline of the wings.

2 Fill a piping bag with the coloured flooding icing and snip the very end of the bag off. Flood the top wings of each butterfly in turn.

3 Use the paintbrush to draw the icing up to the hand-piped line.

4 Pipe small pearls of white icing to form the butterflies' markings. Leave to set for 20 minutes.

5 Flood the bottom wings of each butterfly in turn, and use the paintbrush as before.

6 Add each butterfly's markings. Leave to set for 20 minutes.

To assemble, use the piping bag and nozzle to pipe a head and body for each butterfly on top of a cake. Gently peel the butterfly wings off the waxed paper with a small palette knife. Place one wing on either side of the body at an angle. Place a small square of sponge under each wing to prop it up (see p.144). Leave to set for at least 1 hour before removing the sponge squares.

The finished results are shown on the Baskets in Bloom cake on p.146.

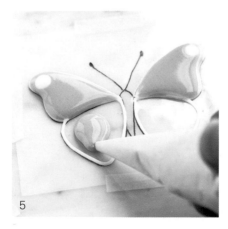

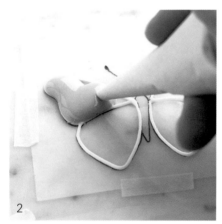

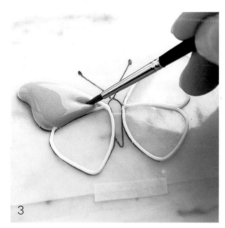

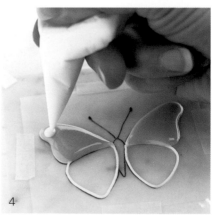

Hand moulding

Hand-moulded decorations can include just about anything, from flowers, animals and insects to boats, cars and figurines. These models are an effective decoration, requiring a set of professional tools and nimble fingers. The beauty is that the models can be made well in advance and lifted onto the covered cake, allowing the decorator to build up confidence. I have included hand-moulded roses, bumble bees and ladybirds in this masterclass section, as they can be used on so many cake designs – from cup cakes to crown cakes, single-tier party cakes to fully tiered wedding cakes. You will find more specific projects using hand moulding in the Cake Gallery section.

You can use sugar paste to make the hand-moulded roses in this section, but for finer-detailed or much larger models, use petal paste (also known as modelling paste). This is similar to sugar paste, with the addition of gum tragacanth, which allows the paste to be rolled or handled in a much thinner and finer form than usual, and sets really firm very quickly. Petal paste can be bought from specialist cake decorating stores. Alternatively, add 1 tsp gum tragacanth powder to 100g (3¹/₂oz) sugar paste and knead well.

The paste will need to be kept in a sealed freezer bag when not being used to prevent it from drying out. Use white fat, or shortening, such as Trex, on your fingertips if the paste is a little dry or crumbly.

Invest in a set of modelling tools – these include a ball tool, markers, a smiley tool, a pokey tool, a foam pad, a friller, some sugar glue, paintbrushes and scissors.

For light dusting, make a small dusting bag using a square of muslin filled with a mixture of icing sugar combined with cornflour, tied up with an elastic band.

Hand-moulded rose

Once mastered, this method of making a hand-moulded rose is quick and easy, and you should be able to make a rose in less than 1 minute! The method here refers only to making sugar paste roses, but you can use the same method for making chocolate plastique or petal paste roses. Sugar paste roses are perfect for crown cakes or larger cakes where they are actually going to be eaten. Chocolate plastique roses can be made in white, milk or dark chocolate plastique. You could even try making the centre petals with darker shades and use lighter shades on the outside. Petal paste roses are for more delicate decorations and, whilst more refined, will be too hard and brittle to consume. If making petal paste roses, use no more than 50g (2oz) at a time. See overleaf for the full process. For a spectacular finishing touch, these roses, which can be made in varying sizes, can all be sprayed and then dredged in edible glitter.

You will need:
- sugar paste, as follows:
  for a 6cm (2½in) diameter rose: 50g (2oz)
  for a 3cm (1¼in) diameter rose: 25g (1oz)
  for a 2cm (¾in) diameter rose: 15g (½oz)
- icing sugar, for dusting

Equipment:
- knife
- A4 plastic document holder cut open on 3 sides with a pair of scissors or knife

On a clean worktop, knead the sugar paste until pliable but not soft and warm. Work on a piece of paste weighing no more than 150g (5½oz) at a time, and keep the remainder in a sealed polythene bag to prevent it drying out. The paste should be gently tacky but not sticky. Use the icing sugar to dust sparingly if the paste is particularly warm and sticking.

Use the whole flat of your hand to roll it into a sausage – the diameter should be 1.5cm (1⅝in) for a small rose, 2.5cm (1in) for medium and 4cm (1½in) for large.

1 Trim the end with a sharp knife and set aside. Cut 6 discs per rose from the sausage – the thickness for each should be 4mm (⅛in), regardless of the size of the finished rose.

2 Open the plastic document holder and lay the 6 discs down with the straight edge facing you and the rounded edges facing away. Replace the cover of the pouch over the discs.

3 With the base of your thumb, gently and quickly press each disc just once to begin to flatten them slightly. (You will need to work fairly swiftly to prevent the paste from drying out and cracking.)

4 To thin the petals, start at the base side of each petal, smoothing your thumb around the curved edge of the petal in a smooth motion. Leave the flat base of each petal untouched.

5 Gently lift up the plastic and look for the smallest petal.

6 Using your thumb, gently rub the petal, starting from the thick, chunky base, to release it from the plastic.

7 As the petal comes away, turn it over so it naturally curls away from you, and lay it over your first finger. The thinner, rounded petal part should be facing away from you over your finger, while the thicker, chunky base rests this side of your finger, parallel to your finger.

8–9 Starting on one side of the petal, gently roll it, curling it up horizontally across your finger inwards to form the centre of the rose.

10 Rub the second petal off the plastic in the same way and lay it over your finger. Lay the seam or join of the central rose in contact with the second petal, so that the top of the central rose is halfway down the second petal. (Do not be tempted to lay the central rose too high.)

11 Gently pinch the second petal around the base of the central rose. Use your finger to gently press and shape the outer edge of the second petal down.

12 Repeat with the third petal, laying the seam of the second petal in the centre of the third petal, so the top of the rose is halfway down the third petal.

13 Pinch around the base and gently shape the petal.

14–17 The final 3 petals form the outer layer of the rose. Lay, pinch and shape them in exactly the same way, so that each covers one third of the outer layer of the rose.

18 Use a sharp knife to slice the chunky base off the rose and set aside on a cake board to firm for about 2 hours.

TO STORE The roses can be kept safely in an airtight container at room temperature for up to 3 months.

You will need:
- yellow sugar paste
- white petal paste
- ½ tsp black colour dust
- 1 tsp dipping alcohol
- white royal icing
- black royal icing (see p.77–8)

Equipment:
- small rolling pin
- smiley tool
- 1cm (³/₈in) single petal cutter
- paintbrush
- piping bags
- 2 no. 1.5 icing nozzles

Bumble bee

These bumble bees are very cute. They can be made well in advance and used to add the finishing detail to a number of cakes.

Roll a hazelnut-size piece of yellow sugar paste into a ball, and elongate slightly. Use the smiley tool to create a smile on one end. Roll out the white petal paste very finely and cut out 2 wings per bumble bee with the petal cutter.

Paint 3 or 4 black stripes around the bumble bee's body, using the black colour dust dissolved in some dipping alcohol. Pipe a small blob of white royal icing on the top of the bumble bee and fix both wings into position. Pipe 2 small white pearls for eyes and leave to set slightly before adding a smaller black pearl on each eye.

Leave to dry for approximately 30 minutes.

You will need:
• red petal paste
• black colour dust
• dipping alcohol
• white royal icing

Equipment:
• line-marking tool
• paintbrush
• piping bag
• no. 1.5 icing nozzle

Ladybird

Like the bumble bees, these ladybirds are cute and can be used to dress individual cakes, larger cakes or cup cakes.

Roll a small fingernail-sized piece of red petal paste into a ball and elongate slightly to one tapered end.

Use the line-marking tool to indent a line the length of the ladybird.

Dissolve some black colour dust in some dipping alcohol, then paint 6 black spots on the ladybird's back.

Paint the blunter end black for the face.

Pipe 2 small white pearls for eyes. Leave to dry for approximately 30 minutes.

Cutters

There are many cutters available, so it is worth building up your collection because you will need them. I have focused on cutters to create different flowers and leaves in this section. Some will cut out one petal at a time, some will cut out a number of petals, and others can cut petals and indent veins and other detail all at the same time. These flowers will be more refined, but I have chosen not to wire them, making them faster to create and safer to include on cakes.

Leaves

There are many leaf cutters available, but I like to use ones that indent the detail onto the leaf at the same time as cutting and pressing them out. They are available in various sizes.

1 Knead the green petal paste until smooth and pliable. Dust the worktop lightly with icing sugar. Roll the petal paste out to a thickness of 1–2mm (1/8in). Place the leaf cutter on the paste and press the base to cut out the leaf.

2 Press the top of the cutter to indent the veining detail onto the leaf. Release.

3 Lift the cutter with the leaf still inside, then press the top again to push the leaf out of the cutter.

4 Hold the leaf and gently twist to create form and texture. Leave on some non-stick paper for 1 hour to dry and firm.

You will need:
- green petal paste
- icing sugar, for dusting

Equipment:
- small rolling pin
- leaf plunger cutter
- non-stick paper

Plunger flowers

These blossoms are great as small filler flowers to add the finishing touch to christening cakes, crown cakes and Easter garlands. They can be made from sugar paste or petal paste in every colour, with hand-piped centres in a contrasting colour. Make these up well in advance and keep them stored in an airtight container.

1 Knead the lilac sugar paste until smooth and pliable. Dust the worktop lightly with icing sugar. Roll out the paste to a thickness of 2mm (⅛in). Place the cutter on the paste and press the base to cut out the flower.

2 Lift the cutter away from the paste with the flower still intact. Place on the top of a clean sponge and press the top of the plunger to remove the flower and form the petals at the same time.

3 Leave on some non-stick paper for 1 hour to dry and firm. Fit the piping bag with the icing nozzle and fill with white royal icing. Ice a centre to each flower.

You will need:
• lilac sugar paste (see p.68)
• icing sugar, for dusting
• 1 quantity white royal icing (see p.77)

Equipment:
• small rolling pin
• 3.5cm (1½in) flower plunger cutter
• sponge
• non-stick paper
• piping bag
• no. 1.5 icing nozzle

Large open roses

Each layer of these petal-paste roses has to be moulded and shaped with a ball tool. Although they are time consuming to make, the result is a delicate, refined open rose that will decorate the finest of cakes

You will need:
- red petal paste
- icing sugar, for dusting
- sugar glue
- black royal icing (see pp.77—8)

Equipment:
- small rolling pin
- 5-petal cutters: 3cm (1¼in), 4.5cm (1¾in) and 6cm (2½in) in diameter
- foam pad
- ball tool
- aluminium foil
- piping bag
- no. 1.5 icing nozzle

1 Knead the red petal paste until smooth and pliable. Dust the worktop lightly with icing sugar. Roll the petal paste out to a thickness of 2mm (⅛in). Cut out a small, medium and large 5-petal rose shape.

2 Place each rose shape in turn on the foam pad. Use the ball tool to gently thin, shape and form each petal on all the rose shapes.

3 Starting with the largest rose shape, place it on some crinkled aluminium foil to give the flower a sense of movement.

4 Brush a small amount of sugar glue in the centre of the rose.

5 Fix the medium-size rose on top, giving it a turn so it sits between the larger petals.

6 Finally, add the smallest rose on top. Fit the piping bag with the icing nozzle and fill with black royal icing. Hand-pipe a small black pearl into the centre of the rose. Leave the rose on the foil for 2 hours to dry and firm before using.

Poppies / Frilly roses

These open poppies can also be adapted for a frilly rose. Smaller than the open rose, they are delicate and quick to make. Add a piped centre, glitter pearl or painted detail to vary the flowers.

You will need:
- red petal paste
- icing sugar, for dusting
- sugar glue
- black petal paste

Equipment:
- small rolling pin
- 3.5cm (1½in) 5-petal flower cutter
- foam pad
- ball tool
- pokey tool
- baking parchment

1 Knead the red petal paste until smooth and pliable. Dust the worktop lightly with icing sugar. Roll out the petal paste to a thickness of 2mm (⅛in). Cut out 2 flowers with the cutter.

2 Place the flowers on the foam pad. Use a ball tool to thin the petal edges and shape the flowers.

3 Brush one of the flowers with sugar glue.

4 Position the second flower on top of the first, ensuring the petals sit between the petals on the base flower.

5 Roll a small pea-sized piece of black petal paste and flatten slightly. Fix in the centre of the flower with sugar glue and use the pokey tool to indent over the surface.

6 Leave the poppy on some baking parchment for 1 hour to dry and firm before using.

Daffodils

Daffodils are the perfect flowers to make for all your spring cakes. Their three-dimensional shape is impressive, adding texture to crown cakes and larger cakes alike.

1 Knead the yellow petal paste until smooth and pliable. Dust the worktop lightly with icing sugar. Roll the paste out to a thickness of 2mm (¹⁄₈in). Cut out 2 petal layers and one trumpet shape with the daffodil cutter.

2 Place the pieces on the foam pad. Use the small ball tool to thin the petal edges and to thin and frill the longer curved edge of the daffodil trumpet.

3 Lift the daffodil trumpet and roll it up, with the frilled edge facing upwards.

4 Fit the piping bag with the icing nozzle and fill with yellow royal icing. Fix the 2 petal layers together with some icing, ensuring the upper layer sits between the petals on the base layer. Pipe a pearl of icing in the centre of the upper layer.

5 Fix the daffodil trumpet into position in the centre of the daffodil. Leave on some non-stick paper for 1 hour to dry and firm.

You will need:
- yellow petal paste
- icing sugar, for dusting
- yellow royal icing (see pp. 77–8)

Equipment:
- small rolling pin
- 3.5cm (1½in) daffodil cutter
- foam pad
- small ball tool
- piping bag
- no. 1.5 icing nozzle
- non-stick paper

Buttercups

These cheerful petal-paste buttercups would look perfect on an Easter cake, cute crown cakes or little girl's christening cake. They can be prepared well in advance and dusted with a little yellow glitter for added sparkle.

1 Assemble the yellow petal paste (which should be kneaded until smooth and pliable), the icing sugar and sugar glue, along with all the equipment.

2 Dust the worktop lightly with icing sugar. Roll the paste out to a thickness of 2mm (1/8in). Cut out a 5-petal shape and a plunger flower for each flower required and place on the foam pad. Use the ball tool to shape each petal gently so that they are nicely curved.

3 Brush the centre of the 5-petal shape with some sugar glue and place the plunger flower centrally on top. Leave on some baking parchment for 1 hour to dry and firm.

You will need:
- yellow petal paste
- icing sugar, for dusting
- sugar glue

Equipment:
- small rolling pin
- 2.5cm (1in) 5-petal flower cutter
- 1cm (3/8in) flower plunger cutter
- foam pad
- ball tool
- baking parchment

Ribbons

Ribbons can add dramatic effect to a cake and provide the finishing touch. Single satin ribbon (shiny on one side) is perfect for edging base boards. Double satin (shiny on both sides) is ideal for surrounding the base of cakes and for ribbon bows, ribbon insertion and wired ribbon loops. Grosgrain (a ribbed matt finish) works well with chocolate-covered cakes but is not suitable for ribbon loops. Organza (sheer and transparent) adds a delicate touch between flowers or tied around the centre of cakes. It should not be used to edge base boards or to seal around the base edge of a cake. It is perfect for wired ribbon loops.

Ribbon bows

You will need:
• ribbon

Equipment:
• small, sharp scissors

Double satin ribbons give the best results for these ribbon bows.

1 Make a loop at the end of a length of ribbon so the shorter tail is positioned away from you and held between your thumb and first or second finger. This will become the right-hand loop of the finished ribbon bow.

2 Bring the long tail over your thumb and round the back of the loop with your other hand. The loop over the thumb will become the centre tie holding the bow together.

3 Push the back of the long tail through the centre tie that is resting over your thumb.

4 As the ribbon comes through the centre tie, it will form the left-hand loop of the ribbon bow.

5 Hold the left-hand loop and tail in your left hand and the right-hand loop and tail in your right hand, and pull taut to form a neat bow.

6 Hold the centre tie and pull each tail to make the loops smaller, neater and even.

7 Trim the tails to the desired length.

Ribbon insertion

You will need:
• ribbon

Equipment:
• tracing paper and fine-liner pen
• pokey tool
• ribbon insertion tool
• small sharp scissors

Ribbon insertion is a clever technique to create the illusion that a ribbon has been threaded through the sugar paste coat on a cake. A special ribbon insertion tool has 2 blades, which will be used as a pair: a slit-making tool to create the icing slits and an insertion blade to tuck the ribbon in gently on both sides. Work with double satin ribbon in a solid contrasting colour for best effect. Top the ribbon insertion loops with handmade bows made from the same ribbon, if desired.

1 Trace the template of the desired design and transfer it onto the cake using the pokey tool.

2 Cut a length of ribbon into little strips each approximately 1.5cm (⅝in) in length.

3 Following the marked design, insert the slit-making tool through the layer of sugar paste, then remove it. Place the left side of the marker tool in the right-hand slit just created to make sure you keep the spacing even as you work around the cake.

4 To insert the ribbon, hold a cut strip of ribbon in your left hand with one edge of the ribbon held at the left slit. Use the insertion tool to push the ribbon into the pre-cut slit until it is secured.

5 Direct the other end of the ribbon to the adjoining slit and use the insertion tool to push this edge securely into the pre-cut slit. Repeat all the way around the cake.

TIPS Cut the ribbon strips as evenly as possible when preparing them.

Ensure the loops are even either by pushing the ribbon in more firmly if a loop looks too loose, or gently pulling a loop out if it is too taut.

If you are making ribbon bows to match the insertion, make these first, so that you can snip the discarded tail cut-offs into strips to be used for insertion.

You will need:
- ribbon
- 28-gauge white wires cut to 15cm (⅝in) length
- white floristry tape

Equipment:
- small, sharp scissors

Ribbon loops (wired)

Wired ribbon loops can be used to complete a floral display, as they will fill gaps between more fragile, brittle sugar flowers. Use a combination of double satin and organza ribbons in different widths and colours to give your cakes maximum impact.

1 Make a loop approximately 10cm (4in) high at the end of a length of ribbon, so the shorter tail is positioned away from you and held between your thumb and first finger.

2 Fold the longer length of ribbon back on itself to create a second loop the same size as the first.

3 Repeat this step to create a third ribbon loop.

4 Fold the ribbon back again as if to start a fourth loop, but cut the ribbon as a single length only, to create a 10cm (4in) tail.

5 Place a length of wire behind and at the base of the ribbon loops – with approximately 2cm (¾in) of wire protruding.

6 Fold this shorter length of wire back on itself.

7 Twist the shorter end tightly around the longer length of wire.

8 Bend the twisted wire down so the ribbon loop becomes the top.

9 Pass a length of white floristry tape behind the twisted wire.

10 Pull the tape taut to cover the ribbon twist and the base of the ribbon loops together.

11 Seal the tape against the wire approximately 5cm (2in) down.

7

8

9

10

11

Hand painting

Hand painting onto cakes covered with sugar paste can be a wonderful way of creating a really individual cake, as no two will ever be the same. For me, this process combines two passions: cake decorating and painting. Our students create wonderful designs when we hold hand-painting masterclasses, as the technique is less foreign to them than piping – they are more comfortable and confident handling a paintbrush than a piping bag.

Take inspiration from nature, textiles and books to design the initial concept. Build up the layers of paint using melted cocoa butter and colour dusts to create an oil-painting effect, which sits on the surface of the cake. Hand painting can be free-flowing, as you add and blend colours, finishing the design with precision detail where necessary.

Cocoa butter, which comes in buttons, is available from specialist cake-decorating stores and online. It keeps for 12 months in an airtight container. Colour dusts come in a wide spectrum of colours – usually in phials or pots. It is essential to include white and black.

Invest in a collection of paintbrushes: larger heads for building up the base colour, and an assortment, varying from medium to fine heads, for adding precision detail.

Place a few buttons of cocoa butter on a saucer suspended over a bowl of boiling water. Position little piles of colour dust on the edge of the saucer, around the melted cocoa butter. Blend each colour (and mixtures of colours) with the cocoa butter to achieve the colours you require. The results provide a translucent colour when painted onto sugar paste. Adding white colour dust to the mix will strengthen the colour, so it is bolder.

Reversing the concept can be a nice idea, so colouring the sugar paste used to cover your cake, then painting the design detail in white, which will really stand out well (see the Passion Flower cake on p.198).

If you make a mistake, you can use an absorbent cloth to soak off the paint – or simply wait for it to dry and then paint over it.

Hand painting using colour dusts blended with dipping alcohol can be used to add detail to hand-moulded or cut-out flowers, insects and models. The painted detail dries much faster, soaking into the icing to create added interest (see the Summer Butterflies cake on p.144).

Hand painting clear edible gel or metallic lustres onto pearls and scrolls or chocolate flowers adds the finishing touch for a truly professional cake. (see the Purlesque cake on p.120).

You will need:
- colour dusts in red, black, white and burgundy

Equipment:
- tracing paper and fine-liner pen
- non-toxic pencil (optional)
- pokey tool
- paintbrushes in various sizes

1 Trace the design on p.214 using the fine-liner pen, and transfer it onto the cake using the pokey tool. Alternatively, lightly sketch the roses on to cake with the non-toxic pencil.

2 Beginning with the largest paintbrush and the red colour dust, paint the background of each rose onto the cake.

3 Leave to set briefly, then start again from the beginning, changing brushes as you build up layers of more red and darker burgundy with soft, circular, sweeping brush strokes.

4 Using another brush, blend the black paint with the red, then add a centre to each rose and more brush strokes on the petals.

5 Finish by highlighting each rose with a swirl of white brush strokes, using the finest brush.

6 Leave the painting to dry.

Cake Gallery

Welcome to the Cake Gallery. The collection of cakes
in this section will feature techniques I have covered in the
Masterclass, with additional skills specific to each design. Whether
you want to create a selection of beautiful afternoon tea cakes, a fun
birthday cake or a stunning four-tier wedding cake adorned with
flowers and painted couture roses, my intention has been to give
you a number of designs aimed at putting all your new skills into
practice. Many of these designs are interchangeable, and I would
encourage you to experiment to create your own cakes using these
designs as inspiration.

Purlesque

I love the simplicity of this cake – but you shouldn't underestimate just how long it takes to decorate. No two pearls are touching, apart from the ring around the base of each tier. The inspiration came from a clustered Chanel pearl necklace. It is a wonderful challenge for the beginner and more accomplished cake decorator alike to perfect their pearls.

a

b

Decorating the cake

1 Fit the piping bags with the different sized nozzles and fill with the royal icings as follows: caramel: large and small; white: large and medium; ivory: medium and small. Pipe a row of pearls around the base of each tier to seal the cake. Place all the bags in a sealed freezer bag while you use the no. 3 nozzle with white.

2 Starting with the top tier, pipe perfect, large, random white pearls over the tier and down the sides. Use a paintbrush to remove any peaks as necessary – although once the cake is fully encrusted with pearls and they have been glazed, these are unlikely to be as noticeable.

3 Move onto the next piping bag, with a different colour, and add extra

pearls over the top and sides of the cake, making sure they do not directly touch any of the white pearls.

4 Continue building up the design with more pearls in different shades and different sizes until the cake is fully encrusted (a). I chose to peter out the pearls slightly as I worked my way down the cake, but you may prefer not to.

5 Brush the white pearls with clear edible gel. Mix some topaz lustre with dipping alcohol and brush a selection of the ivory pearls with topaz lustre. Next, mix some topaz and gold lustre together with some more dipping alcohol and brush this over a selection of the caramel pearls (b).

Preparing the cake

Place the cakes on the cake boards of the same size and cover with a base coat of your choice, as shown on p.71 and the ivory sugar paste top coat, as shown on p.72. Line the base board with ivory sugar paste, as shown on p.73, and surround with the ivory ribbon, fixed with glue. Leave the cakes and base board to dry overnight.

Fix the base tier centrally into position on the base board with royal icing. Dowel and direct stack the tiers, using 6 dowels per tier, as shown on p.83. Place the cake on a turntable.

You will need:
- 10cm (4in), 15cm (6in), 20cm (8in) and 25cm (10in) round cakes
- 10cm (4in), 15cm (6in), 20cm (8in) and 25cm (10in) thick round cake boards
- marzipan, sugar paste or white chocolate plastique, for the base coat (see pp.71 and 72 for quantities)
- ivory sugar paste (see p.68), for the top coat (see p.72 for quantities)
- 36cm (14in) round base board
- ivory sugar paste, for the base board (see p.72 for quantity)
- 1.15m (3ft 9in) ivory ribbon, 15mm (5/8in) wide
- 18 dowelling rods
- 2 quantities royal icing, divided between 3 bowls and one coloured ivory, one caramel and one left white (see pp.77–8)
- clear edible gel
- topaz and gold lustres
- dipping alcohol

Equipment:
- small sharp scissors
- glue stick
- turntable
- 6 piping bags
- 2 no. 1.5 icing, 2 no. 2 and 2 no. 3 icing nozzles
- paintbrush

Art Nouveau

The Art Nouveau era at the start of the 20th century, with its fluid, floaty and asymmetrical style, was the precursor to the Art Deco era of symmetry and angular graphic designs. This delicate cake, highlighting swirls and pearls, and with a simple blossom on the top, would be perfect for a baby shower, christening or birthday cake.

Preparing the cake

Place the cake on the cake board and cover with a base coat of your choice, as shown on p.71, and the white sugar paste top coat, as shown on p.72. Surround the cake with the 25mm (1in) ribbon and fix and fix with a dab of royal icing. Cover the base board with white sugar paste, as shown on p.73. Surround the board with the 15mm (5/8in) pink ribbon, fixed into position with glue. Leave the cake and the base board to dry overnight. Place the cake on the lined base board.

You will need:

- 10cm (4in) round cake
- 10cm (4in) thick round cake board
- marzipan, sugar paste or white chocolate plastique, for the base coat (see pp.71 and 72 for quantity)
- white sugar paste, for the top coat (see p.72 for quantity)
- 35cm (14in) pink ribbon, 25mm (1in) wide
- 15cm (6in) round base board
- white sugar paste, for the base board (see p.72 for quantity)
- 55cm (22in) pink ribbon, 15mm (5/8in) wide
- 1 quantity royal icing, divided into 2 bowls and one coloured pale pink and one green (see pp.77–8)
- white open petal paste poppy-style flower with a hand-piped pink centre (see p.107)

Equipment:

- glue stick
- tracing paper and fine-liner pen
- pokey tool
- 2 piping bags
- no. 1.5 icing nozzle

Decorating the cake
1 Trace the design on p.219 and transfer it onto the top and sides of the cake, using the pokey tool.

2 Fit a piping bag with the icing nozzle and fill with pink icing. Pipe a fine trail, allowing the icing to fall into position on the cake.

3 Build up a delicate row of pearls along the top edge of the hand-piped line.

4 Repeat, but this time add the pearls along the underside edge of the line.

5 Pipe the next line using the same-size nozzle and piping bag to build up the design, covering the indent created by the pokey tool.

6 Finish with a single row of pearls around the cake directly above the ribbon.

7 Fill the second piping bag with the green royal icing, snip the end as shown on p.93 and pipe 3 green leaves in the centre. Place the the white poppy-style flower on the leaves and leave to set overnight.

Pretty in Pink

I can picture this cake at a Cinderella-style wedding. Feminine, pretty and pink, it bedazzles with pink glitter sparkles and delicate white hand-piped pearls. As a chic alternative, substitute the pink with a warm caramel colour icing and use coffee, chocolate or date cake inside.

You will need:

- 10cm (4in), 15cm (6in) (cut to 5cm/2in deep), 20cm (8in) and 25cm (10in) round cakes
- 10cm (4in), 15cm (6in), 20cm (8in) and 25cm (10in) thick round cake boards
- marzipan, sugar paste or white chocolate plastique, for the base coat (see pp.71 and 72 for quantities)
- white sugar paste, for the top coat on the 10cm (4in) and 20cm (8in) cakes and for the base board (see p.72 for quantities), plus 250g (9oz) for the ring and dome
- pink sugar paste (see p.68), for the top coat on the 15cm (6in) and 25cm (10in) cakes (see p.72 for quantities)
- 33cm (13in) round base board
- 3.6m (12ft) white grosgrain ribbon, 15mm (5/8in) wide
- 20 dowelling rods
- 1 quantity white royal icing (see p.77)
- 15cm (6in) round polystyrene block, 5cm (2in) deep
- 30cm (12in) pink ribbon, 25mm (1in) wide
- 1 quantity pink royal icing (see pp.77–8)
- 18 pink open roses, dusted with glitter (see p.106)
- triple ribbon loops with tails (see p.112–13), as follows:

    10 pink loops using 8m (26ft) ribbon, 15mm (5/8in) wide

    10 pink loops using 8m (26ft) ribbon, 25mm (1in) wide

    10 white organza loops using 8m (26ft) ribbon, 25mm (1in) wide

Equipment:

- small sharp scissors
- glue stick
- tracing paper and fine-liner pen
- pokey tool
- ruler
- 4 piping bags
- no. 3, 2 and 1.5 icing nozzles
- paintbrush

Preparing the cake

Place the cakes on the cake boards of the same size and cover with a base coat of your choice, as shown on p.71. Then cover the 10cm (4in) and 20cm (8in) cakes with white sugar paste and the 15cm (6in) and 25cm (10in) cakes with pink sugar paste, as shown on p.72. Line the base board with white sugar paste, as shown on p.73, and surround with 1.1m (3ft 8in) of the white grosgrain ribbon, fixed with glue. Leave the cakes and board to dry overnight.

Dowel and direct stack the top 3 tiers, using 6 dowels per tier, as shown on p.83. Fix the base tier centrally into position on the base board with white royal icing and prepare it for blocking, as shown on p.82, using the remaining 8 dowels. Surround all the tiers with the remaining white ribbon, and fix into position with a dab of royal icing.

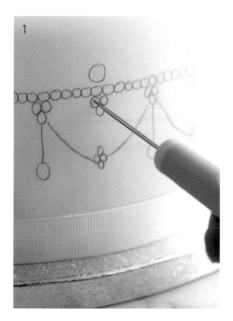

Decorating the cake

1 Trace the template on p.216 and transfer it onto the white tiers with the pokey tool, lined up just above the ribbon.

2 Fit 3 of the piping bags with an icing nozzle and fill with some of the white royal icing. Starting with the top tier, use the no. 3 nozzle to pipe the top row of pearls, plus the extra intermittent row above and the large pearl at the base of the vertical strands of pearls. Use the no. 2 nozzle to pipe the clusters of 3 pearls (picots) and 4 pearls (diamante).

3 Finally, use the no. 1.5 nozzle to pipe the chains and pearl drops.

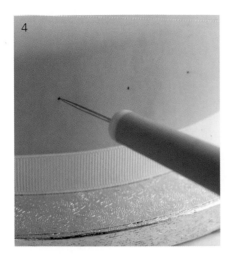

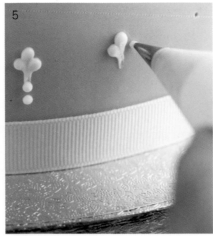

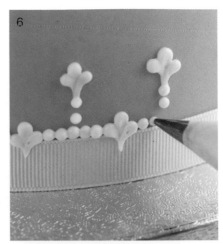

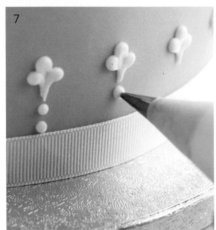

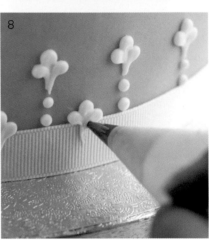

4 On the second tier (pink), use a ruler and pokey tool to mark every 3cm (1¼in), 15mm (⅝in) above the ribbon, where each of the fleur de lys designs will be piped

5 Pipe the design using the no. 2 nozzle, with 2 pearls below.

6 Pipe a fleur de lys design between the first row, sitting directly on the ribbon. Join these fleurs de lys with a chain of pearls piped with the no. 2 nozzle.

7 Repeat the design from the first (white) tier onto the third (white) tier. Then repeat the design from the second (pink) tier onto the base (pink) tier.

8 Concentrate on just piping a fleur de lys design on the base-tier ribbon, omitting the chain of pearls. Leave to dry overnight.

Dressing the cake

9 Surround the polystyrene block with the 25mm (1in) pink ribbon and fix with glue. To assemble, place the polystyrene block on the base tier, fixed with some royal icing, and fix the 3 stacked tiers in position on top.

10 Roll 200g (7oz) of the remaining white sugar paste into a ring. Dampen the top of the base tier 2cm (¾in) inside the cake with a moistened paint-brush and fix the ring into position as shown on p.201.

11 Fill a piping bag with pink royal icing and pipe a blob on the white sugar-paste ring. Fix the first open rose into position at an angle to bridge the gap between the third and base tiers. Fix a thin pink ribbon loop next to the open rose by pushing it into the sugar-paste ring.

12 Add a thicker pink ribbon loop and then a white organza ribbon loop in a similar way to fill the space, then butt the next open rose up against them, fixed into position with royal icing. Continue to work around the tier until full.

13 Use the remaining 50g (2oz) pink sugar paste to create a dome for the top tier and fix into position with a little water. Push 3 pink ribbon loops into a triangular position in the dome and fix 3 pink glitter open roses between the loops with royal icing. Build up the top decoration with the remaining ribbon loops. Use the sharp scissors to snip the ribbon loop tails at a nice angle to complete the decoration.

Hello, Dolly!

I was inspired by the classic film *Hello, Dolly!* to design this majestic wedding cake. As Mrs Dolly Levi makes her entrance to the Harmonia Gardens, she stands silently, with awesome presence, at the top of the sweeping red staircase wearing a gorgeous gold brocade and sequin dress, and her auburn hair is finished with yellow ochre and sage green feathers. This stunning cake commands the same centre of attention, deserving its place as the focal point at the finest of weddings.

Preparing the cake

Place the cakes on the cake boards of the same size and cover with a base coat of your choice, as shown on p.71, and the gold sugar paste top coat, as shown on p.72. Brush some gold lustre over the cakes (a).

Line the base boards with gold sugar paste, as shown on p.73, then brush with gold lustre. Surround the base boards with the 15mm (5/8in) gold ribbon and fix with the glue stick. Leave the cakes and base boards to dry overnight.

Decorating the cake

1 Trace the Hello, Dolly! template on p.218 and transfer it onto each tier with the pokey tool, starting from the top and working downwards (b).

2 Fix the base tier centrally into position on the smaller base board with a dab of royal icing, then fix the smaller base board to the larger one. Prepare the base tier to be blocked, as shown on p.82, using 8 dowels. Surround all the tiers with the 25mm (1in) gold ribbon, fixed into position with royal icing. Use the remaining 30cm (12in) ribbon to surround the polystyrene block and fix with glue.

You will need:

- 10cm (4in), 15cm (6in), 20cm (8in) and 25cm (10in) round cakes
- 10cm (4in), 15cm (6in), 20cm (8in) and 25cm (10in) thick round cake boards
- marzipan, sugar paste or white chocolate plastique, for the base coat (see pp.71 and 72 for quantities)
- gold sugar paste (see p.68), for the top coat (see p.72 for quantities) and the base boards (see p.73 for quantities), plus an extra 250g (9oz) for the ring and dome
- gold lustre
- 33cm (13in) and 40cm (16in) round base boards
- 2.4m (8ft) gold ribbon, 15mm (5/8in) wide
- 2 quantities gold royal icing (see pp.77–8)
- 20 dowelling rods
- 2.8m (9ft) gold ribbon, 25mm (1in) wide
- 15cm (6in) round polystyrene block, 5cm (2in) deep
- dipping alcohol
- 18 open roses (see p.106), made with gold petal paste and finished with sage-green pearl centres
- triple ribbon loops with tails (see pp.112–13), as follows:
    10 sage-green loops using 8m (26ft) ribbon, 15mm (5/8in) wide
    10 rust-orange organza loops using 8m (26ft) ribbon, 9mm (3/8in) wide
    10 red organza loops using 8m (26ft) ribbon, 25mm (1in) wide

Equipment:

- paintbrush
- small sharp scissors
- glue stick
- tracing paper and fine-liner pen
- pokey tool
- piping bag
- no. 3 icing nozzle
- turntable

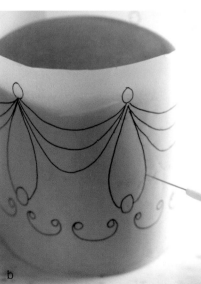

c

d

3 Fit a piping bag with the icing nozzle and fill with gold royal icing. Place the top tier onto a turntable and pipe the design as shown (c) (d). Repeat on the second and third tiers. Once all 3 tiers are finished, hand-pipe the base tier in the same way. Set aside and allow all the tiers to dry overnight. Mix some gold lustre with dipping alcohol at a ratio of 1:2 and paint all the hand-piped detail using the paintbrush.

4 To assemble, dowel and stack the top 3 tiers as shown on p. 83, using 6 dowels per tier. Add some royal icing to the top of the polystyrene block on the base tier, then fix the 3 stacked tiers in place on top of it.

Dressing the cake

5 Roll 200g (7oz) of the remaining gold sugar paste into a ring, dampen the top of the base tier 2cm (3/4in) inside the cake with a moistened paintbrush, and fix the sugar paste ring into position. Use the final 50g (2oz) of gold sugar paste to create a dome for the top tier and fix into position with a little water.

6 Pipe a blob of icing on the sugar paste ring. Fix the first open rose into position at an angle to bridge the gap between the third and base tiers.

7 Fix the first ribbon loop next to the open rose by pushing it into the sugar paste ring. Add more ribbon loops in a similar way to fill the space, then butt the next open rose up against the ribbons, fixing it into position with royal icing. Continue to work around the space between the tiers until it is filled and there are no gaps (e).

8 For the top tier, push 3 ribbon loops into a triangular position in the gold sugar paste dome and fix 3 gold open roses between the loops with royal icing. Build up the top decoration with the remaining loops. Snip the ribbon loop tails at a nice angle to complete the decoration.

Liberty Flowers

This design was created specifically for renowned department store, Liberty of London, taking inspiration from their neon colours and striking decorations. This design works well with a choice of two colours piped one way and in reverse. We have included fuchsia pink and lime here, but tangerine and fuchsia, navy and aqua or caramel and ivory could all be very effective.

Preparing the cakes

Cover each cake with a base coat of your choice and the white sugar paste top coat, as shown on p.69. Leave overnight to dry. Surround half the cakes with pink ribbon and the other half with green ribbon, and fix into position with a dab of royal icing.

You will need (per cake):
- 5cm (2in) individual round cake (see p.69 for cutting instructions)
- 60g (2½oz) marzipan, sugar paste or white chocolate plastique, for the base coat
- 75g (3oz) white sugar paste, for the top coat
- 20cm (8in) pink or green ribbon, 15mm (⅝in) wide

Plus:
- 1 quantity white royal icing, split into 2 bowls, one coloured fuchsia, the other lime green (see pp.77–8)

Equipment:
- small sharp scissors
- turntable
- pokey tool
- 4 piping bags
- 2 no. 1.5 and no. 2 icing nozzles

Decorating the cakes

1 Place a pink-ribboned cake on a turntable. Use the pokey tool to mark the centre of each cake and the 6 points around the top of the cake where the petals will end (a).

2 Fit a piping bag with a no. 2 nozzle and fill with half the fuchsia pink royal icing. Starting at the centre of the cake, pipe the first loop to the edge of the cake and back to the centre (b). Turn the cake around and pipe the second loop directly opposite the first. Turn the cake and pipe 2 loops between the first and second, then spin the cake around and pipe the final 2 loops between the first and second on the opposite side, so you end up with 6 loops in total.

3 Fit another piping bag with a no. 1.5 nozzle and fill with half the lime green royal icing. Pipe small lines of green icing between each pink loop to the edge of the cake (c).

4 Finish by piping a pearl of green icing in the centre of the decoration (d).

5 Decorate all the pink-ribboned cakes in this colourway, then switch the colours around and pipe the green-ribboned cakes with thicker green loops and thinner pink lines and central pearl, using the other 2 piping bags and icing nozzles.

Purple Azalea Lace

This cake has been surrounded with deep purple ribbon, decorated with our hand-piped Little Venice Cake Company lace design and finished with rows of open azaleas with hand-piped pearls. This contemporary wedding cake combines pressure piping in a bold purple colour, with the azalea-style roses. Less forgiving than hand piping in white, this technique will certainly test your skills. I have chosen to use a wide ribbon around the base of each tier to frame the azaleas and to still allow the hand piping to be fully appreciated. To make the tiers super deep, with an overall height of 10cm (4in), each cake is placed on a 2.5cm (1in) deep polystyrene dummy of the same size as the cake before covering.

You will need:
- 15cm (6in), 20cm (8in) and 25cm (10in) round cakes
- 15cm (6in), 20cm (8in) and 25cm (10in) round polystyrene dummies, 2.5cm (1in) deep
- marzipan, sugar paste or white chocolate plastique, for the base coat (see pp.71 and 72 for quantities)
- white sugar paste, for the top coat (see p.72 for quantities)
- 33cm (13in) and 40cm (16in) round base boards
- purple sugar paste (see p.68) for the base boards (see p.72 for quantities)
- 2.25m (7ft 6in) purple ribbon, 35mm (1½in) wide
- 2.5m (8ft 3in) purple ribbon, 15mm (⅝in) wide
- 1 quantity purple royal icing (see pp.77–8)
- 12 dowelling rods
- 45 white azalea-style roses with purple centres (see the poppy method on p.107)
- 3 fabric azaleas, to dress

Equipment:
- tracing paper and fine-liner pen
- small sharp scissors
- turntable
- pokey tool
- 2 piping bags
- no. 1.5 and no. 2 icing nozzles

Preparing the cake
Place each cake on a same-size polystyrene dummy and cover both the cake and dummy together with a base coat of your choice, as shown on p.71, and the white sugar paste top coat, as shown on p.72. Line the base boards with purple sugar paste, as shown on p.73. Surround all the tiers with 35mm (1½in) purple ribbon, fixed into position with a dab of royal icing, and the base boards with 15mm (⅝in) purple ribbon, fixed with glue. Leave to dry overnight.

a

b

Decorating the cake
1 Trace the LVCC Lace design on p.216 and transfer onto the cakes with the pokey tool as a single row around the base of each tier directly above the ribbon. Place the top tier on a turntable.

2 Fit 1 of the piping bags with the no. 2 nozzle and fill with half the purple royal icing. Pressure-pipe the LVCC lace design (see pp.94–5) around the top tier, before moving on to the middle then base tiers (a). Leave to dry overnight.

3 Fit the second piping bag with the no. 1.5 nozzle and fill with the remaining purple royal icing, then pipe pearls in the centre of each of the azalea-style roses (b). Leave to dry overnight. Dowel and direct stack the top 3 tiers, using 6 dowels per tier, as shown on p.83. Surround each tier with the roses, iced directly on to the deep purple ribbon. Finally, lay the fabric azaleas on the top tier.

Pompadour

I have used a subtle palette of pastel colours for this Pompadour cake and the individual versions overleaf. Delicately coloured and decorated, with a lustred hand-piped design, this chic French-style cake would be lovely for a special dinner party celebration or anniversary.

Preparing the cake

Place the cake on the cake board and cover with a base coat of your choice, as shown on p.71, and the pink sugar paste top coat, as shown on p.72. Surround the cake with the 25mm (1in) ivory ribbon, fixed with a dab of royal icing. Line the base board with the pistachio green sugar paste, as shown on p.73, and surround it with the 15mm (5/8in) ivory ribbon, fixed with glue. Leave the cake and board to dry overnight.

You will need:

- 15cm (6in) square cake
- 15cm (6in) thick square cake board
- marzipan, sugar paste or white chocolate plastique, for the base coat (see pp.71 and 72 for quantity)
- pale pink sugar paste (see p.68), for the top coat (see p.72 for quantity)
- 70cm (28in) ivory grosgrain ribbon, 25mm (1in) wide
- 1 quantity ivory royal icing (see pp.77–8)
- 23cm (9in) square base board
- pistachio green sugar paste (see p.68), for the base board (see p.72 for quantity)
- 95cm (38in) ivory grosgrain ribbon, 15mm (5/8in) wide

- topaz lustre
- dipping alcohol
- single fresh or sugar rose

Equipment:

- small sharp scissors
- glue stick
- sheet of tracing paper cut to the height of the cake and the length of one side
- ruler
- pokey tool
- piping bag
- no. 1.5 icing nozzle
- paintbrush

Decorating the cake

1 Fix the cake centrally into position on the base board with royal icing. Hold the sheet of tracing paper in line with the top edge of the cake and mark 2.5cm (1in) intervals with the pokey tool all around the cake.

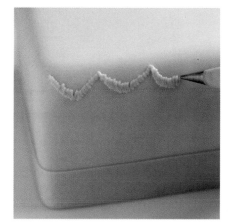

2 Fit the piping bag with the icing nozzle and fill with ivory royal icing. Hold the piping bag at the first point and wiggle your hand up and down to create a scalloped loop to the next marked point. Repeat the design around the cake, keeping the loops even in size.

3 Pipe the bows (see p.92) at the top of each loop, starting at the centre and allowing the line to come out to top right, straight down, then back to the centre, before heading out to top left, straight down, then back to the centre. Pipe the 2 ribbon bow tails. Repeat all the way around.

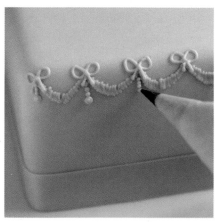

4 Pipe a vertical row of pearls straight down beneath the ribbon bows, with a larger pearl at the base.

5 Underneath the middle of each swag, pipe a triangle of 3, 2, 1 tiny pearls, as shown. Leave to set.

6 Blend some topaz lustre and some dipping alcohol on a 1:2 ratio, and brush over the entire design. Finally, add the rose.

Pompadour Trinkets

The looped design used for the large Pompadour cake (see p.136), transposes well onto these individual trinket cakes. The same design has been piped around the edge of the cakes, with a hand-painted ribbon bow added in the centre. I have used shades of delicate colours that combine so well together.

Preparing the cakes

Cover each cake with a base coat of your choice, as shown on pp.66–7, and one of the sugar paste top coats (pale pink, pistachio green, powder blue or buttermilk), as shown on p.68. Leave overnight to dry. Surround each cake with ivory ribbon, whatever the colour of the sugar paste, and fix into position with a dab of royal icing.

You will need (per cake):
- 4cm (1½in) individual square cake (see p.66 for cutting instructions)
- 60g (2½oz) marzipan, sugar paste or white chocolate plastique, for the base coat
- 75g (3oz) pale pink, pistachio, powder blue or buttermilk sugar paste (see p.68), for the top coat
- 20cm (8in) ivory ribbon, 9mm (³/₈in) wide

Plus:
- 1 quantity ivory royal icing (see p.77–8)
- topaz lustre
- dipping alcohol
- cocoa butter
- black and white colour dust

Equipment:
- small sharp scissors
- piping bag
- tracing paper and fine-liner pen
- pokey tool
- no. 1.5 icing nozzle
- paintbrush

a

b

Decorating the cakes

1 Trace the bow template on p.217 and use the pokey tool to mark it onto the top of each cake (a).

2 Using the pokey tool, mark around the top edge of each cake – at the corners and then two evenly spaced points along each straight side. (Note: I found that these cakes were small enough to mark by eye rather than needing to mark them with tracing paper and a ruler.)

3 Melt the cocoa butter and colour dusts together on a saucer over a saucepan of simmering water. Paint the bow on the top of each cake in white, outlining in black (b).

4 Follow steps 2–6 on p.137, noting that on the trinket cakes the ribbon bows and tails are added only on the corners, not at the top of each swag.

Vintage Chic

This design will really test your hand-piping royal icing skills. The cake is initially covered in royal icing to keep the edges angular, then hand decorated in a white pinstripe design before we switch to a star nozzle for the top piped scrolls and base trail. Chic and elegant, this design transposes well to a tiered cake for a classic wedding. I have dressed this cake with a stunning handmade porcelain peony. Use silk or sugar flowers or simply lay the bridal bouquet next to the cake for maximum effect.

You will need:
- 15cm (6in) square cake
- marzipan, sugar paste or white chocolate plastique, for the base coat (see pp.71 and 72 for quantity)
- royal icing, for the top coat (see p.77 for quantity)
- 23cm (9in) square base board
- 80cm (32in) bridal white grosgrain ribbon, 15mm (5/8in) wide
- 1 quantity white royal icing (see p.77)
- flower(s) of your choice

Equipment:
- glue stick
- 2 piping bags
- no. 3 icing nozzle and no. 5 star icing nozzle

Preparing the cake

Place the cake in the centre of the base board. Cover the cake with panels of a base coat of your choice (marzipan, sugar paste or chocolate plastique), as shown on p.70. Cover the cake and board with the royal icing top coat, as shown on pp.80–81. Surround the base board with the ribbon, fixed in place with the glue stick. Leave the cake and board to dry overnight.

Decorating the cake

1 Fit a piping bag with the no. 3 nozzle and fill with royal icing. Starting 2.5cm (1in) from a corner, pipe the first line vertically, making contact at the top and base of the cake and allowing the line to fall and be pushed into position. (If you look closely, you will see that the piping nozzle and line of icing is almost at right angles to the cake, which is the perfect angle to achieve this technique). Pipe the next line parallel to the first, and continue all the way around the cake. (See p.90 for more detailed instructions.)

2 Fit another piping bag with the no. 5 star nozzle and fill with more royal icing. Starting at one corner of the top, pipe alternating pressure-piped scrolls around the top edge, following the instructions on p.92.

3 Finish by piping a uniform trail of star pearls around the base of the cake, as shown on p.92). Leave to set overnight before dressing with a flower (or flowers) of your choice.

Georgian Lace

Architecture of the Georgian period (1714–1830) is striking for its regal symmetry. This cake has the same formal quality, combining the perfect ivory iced pearls with the repeated black flocking design of our Little Venice Cake Company lace design, and finished with a large double satin ivory ribbon and bow. Simple, striking, flawlessly decorated and set on a black-lined board, this cake exudes class.

You will need:
- 10cm (4in), 15cm (6in), 20cm (8in) and 25cm (10in) square cakes
- 10cm (4in), 15cm (6in), 20cm (8in) and 25cm (10in) thick square cake boards
- marzipan, sugar paste or white chocolate plastique, for the base coat (see pp.71 and 72 for quantities)
- ivory sugar paste (see p.68), for the top coat (see p.72 for quantities)
- 33cm (14in) square base board
- black sugar paste (see p.68), for the base board (see p.72 for quantity)
- 3.5m (11ft 6in) black ribbon, 15mm (⅝in) wide
- 1 quantity royal icing, divided between 2 bowls and one coloured ivory, the other black (see pp.77–8)
- 18 dowelling rods
- 2m (6ft 6in) ivory ribbon, 35mm (1½in) wide

Equipment:
- small sharp scissors
- glue stick
- tracing paper and fine-liner pen
- pokey tool
- 2 piping bags
- nos. 1.5 and 2 icing nozzles
- turntable

a

Preparing the cake
Place the cakes on the cake boards of the same size and cover with a base coat of your choice, as shown on p.71, and the ivory sugar paste top coat, as shown on p.72. Line the base board with black sugar paste, as shown on p.73, and edge it with 1.5m (5ft) of the black ribbon, fixing it with glue. Leave to dry overnight.

Decorating the cake
1 Fix the base tier centrally into position on the base board with a dab of royal icing. Surround the base and the third tier with the remaining black ribbon.

2 Trace the LVCC lace design on p.216 using the tracing paper and pen, and transfer it as a single row around the third tier and a double row around the base tier, using the pokey tool. Place the third tier on a turntable.

3 Fit a piping bag with the no. 2 icing nozzle and fill with black royal icing. Pressure-pipe the LVCC lace design around the cake, as shown on pp.94–5, before moving on to the base tier, piping the upper row first, then finishing with the bottom row (a). Leave to dry overnight.

4 Dowel and direct stack the tiers, using 6 dowels per tier, as shown on p.83. Surround the top 2 tiers with lengths of the ivory ribbon.

5 Fit a piping bag with the no. 1.5 icing nozzle and fill with ivory royal icing. Start icing with the top tier. Pipe a single row of pearls around the cake directly above the ribbon and 3–5mm (⅛–¼in) apart. Pipe the second row 3–5mm (⅛–¼in) above the first row, spaced between the pearls of the first row. Repeat until all the sides of the cake are covered, then repeat on the second tier, keeping the rows straight and the pearls evenly spaced and sized. Leave all the tiers to dry overnight.

Dressing the cake
6 Make a large ribbon bow with the remaining ivory ribbon and fix into position at the base of the second tier.

Summer Butterflies

Sugar butterflies look particularly effective on individual cakes, with their wings iced into position, ready to flutter by. I have hand painted some detail on to these butterflies and added a cluster of flowers to each cake to finish.

Preparing the cakes

Cover each cake with a base coat of your choice and the sugar paste top coat, as shown on p.69. Use tangerine sugar paste for half the cakes and lime green sugar paste for the rest. Leave overnight to dry.

Surround half the cakes with tangerine ribbon and the other half with lime green ribbon, and fix into position with a dab of royal icing.

Make the butterflies following the instructions on p.97, making half with the orange icing and half with the green icing, but with no white markings. Leave to dry for 4 hours.

Blend the orange and green colour dusts separately with some dipping alcohol to different strengths, and brush the colours on to the butterflies' wings to add shading and detail. Leave to dry overnight.

Decorating the cakes

1 To assemble, fit a piping bag with the no. 2 nozzle and fill with white royal icing. Pipe a head and body for each butterfly directly on top of a cake.

2 Gently peel the butterfly wings off the waxed paper with a small palette knife. Place one wing on either side of the body at an angle.

3 Place a small square of sponge under each wing to prop it up. Allow to set for at least 1 hour before removing the sponge squares.

4 Place a butterfly on each cake and fix a cluster of plunger flowers next to it with a little royal icing.

You will need (per cake):

- 5cm (2in) individual round cake (see p.69 for cutting instructions)
- 60g (2½oz) marzipan, sugar paste or white chocolate plastique, for the base coat
- 75g (3oz) tangerine or lime green sugar paste (see p.68), for the top coat
- 20cm (8in) tangerine or lime green ribbon, 15mm (⅝in) wide

Plus:

- 1 quantity royal icing, split into 3 bowls, and one left white, with the remaining 2 thinned to flooding consistency and coloured orange and green (see pp.77–9)
- cake board
- orange and green colour dusts
- dipping alcohol
- assorted plunger flowers (see p.105)

Equipment:

- small sharp scissors
- tracing paper and fine-liner pen
- masking tape
- waxed paper
- 4 piping bags
- no. 1.5 and no. 2 icing nozzles
- paintbrush
- small palette knife
- sponge squares

Baskets in Bloom

This is the perfect cake on which to test all your newly learned skills. The tiers are covered with sugar paste and then hand-piped with this intricate basket-weave design. The tiers are blocked with hand-moulded roses studded with cut-out leaves and flooded butterflies. Impressive, gorgeous, fresh and floral – this is perfect for any summer occasion.

You will need:
- 10cm (4in) and 20cm (8in) round cakes
- 10cm (4in) and 20cm (8in) thick round cake boards
- marzipan, sugar paste or white chocolate plastique, for the base coat (see pp.71 and 72 for quantities)
- white sugar paste, for the top coat and base board (see p.72 for quantities), plus 150g (5oz) for a ring and a dome
- 30cm (12in) round base board
- 1m (39in) green ribbon, 15mm (5⁄8in) wide
- 3 quantities royal icing (see p.77)
- 12cm (5in) thick round cake board
- 6 dowelling rods
- 25 hand-moulded roses in shades of pink and lilac (see pp.99–101), made the day before
- 30 cut-out rose leaves (see p.104), made the day before
- 8–12 run-out butterflies (larger size) (see p.97), made the day before

Equipment:
- glue stick
- 10cm (4in) and 20cm (8in) thick round cake boards (to draw around)
- pokey tool
- 2 piping bags
- no. 3 and no. 19B (basket-weave) icing nozzles
- paintbrush

Preparing the cake

Place the cakes on the cake boards of the same size and cover with a base coat of your choice, as shown on p.71, and the white sugar paste top coat, as shown on p.72. Line the base board with white sugar paste, as shown on p.73, and surround it with green ribbon, fixed with glue. Leave the cakes and base board to dry overnight.

Fix the base tier centrally into position on the base board using some royal icing, and fix the top tier on to the 12cm (5in) thick round cake board in the same way. Mark around the top of both tiers by placing the spare cake boards on top of the cakes and scoring around the edge with a pokey tool.

Decorate each tier with the basket-weave design, using the piping bags and icing nozzles, as shown on p.96. Leave to dry overnight. (Note that you will need to use more of the icing for fixing the elements into position the next day.)

To assemble, dowel the base tier for stacking, and fix the top tier into position. (The deep silver board/drum will still be visible at this stage.)

Decorating the cake

1 Roll 100g (3½oz) of the remaining white sugar paste into a ring that will fit around the top of the base tier, 2cm (¾in) in from the edge. Fix into position with a little water and a paintbrush (a).

2 Pipe a large pearl of royal icing onto the sugar-paste ring (b).

3 Fix the first rose carefully into position (c).

4 Flank this rose with several hand-cut leaves, which can either be pressed directly into the sugar-paste ring or fixed with additional royal icing to secure (d).

5 Carefully ice a flooded butterfly into position next to the flower and leaves. Continue around the cake until all the gaps are filled (e).

6 Mould the remaining 50g (2oz) sugar paste into a dome and fix into position on the top tier. Add roses, leaves and butterflies to the top to dress.

7 Fix the final butterfly, rose and leaves to one side of the base tier.

TIP It is worth making extra butterflies and roses, because some may well break as you are dressing the cake. Any spares can be used to dress the cake table or saved for another occasion.

Candy Cane

These hand-moulded candy canes can be made well in advance of making this cake. They can also be used to decorate individual crown cakes (see p.163), be attached to presents or even hung on a Christmas tree. Here I have added three canes to the top of a cake, and hand-piped a loop design topped with a fleur de lys around the sides six times.

Preparing the cake

Place the cake on the cake board and cover with a base coat of your choice, as shown on p.71, and the white sugar paste top coat, as shown on p.72. Line the base board with red sugar paste topped with glitter, as shown on p.73, and surround it with the 15mm (5/8in) red ribbon, fixed with glue. Leave the cake and board to dry overnight.

Decorating the cake

1 To make the candy canes, knead the red and white sugar pastes separately until smooth and pliable, but not sticky. On a worktop dusted with icing sugar, roll each out to a thin sausage approximately 4–5mm (1/8–1/4in) wide. Line up the red and white strands side by side and hold at both ends. Twist gently in opposite decorations to twist the strands together.

You will need:

- 15cm (6in) round cake
- 15cm (6in) thick round cake board
- marzipan, sugar paste or white chocolate plastique, for the base coat (see pp.71 and 72 for quantity)
- white sugar paste, for the top coat (see p.72 for quantity)
- 23cm (9in) round base board
- red sugar paste (see p.68), for the base board (see p.72 for quantity)
- edible varnish
- edible red glitter
- 80cm (32in) red ribbon, 15mm (5/8in) wide
- 50g (2oz) red sugar paste
- 50g (2oz) white sugar paste
- icing sugar, for dusting
- royal icing, for fixing
- 3 red ribbon bows made with 60cm (24in) red ribbon, 3mm (1/8in) wide (see p.110)
- 55cm (22in) red-and-white polka dot ribbon, 25mm (1in) wide
- 1 quantity red royal icing (see pp.77–8)

Equipment:

- small sharp scissors
- glue stick
- ruler
- sharp knife
- non-stick paper
- 2 piping bags
- tracing paper and fine-liner pen
- pokey tool
- no. 2 icing nozzle

2

2 Place your hands on top and press down while rolling to seal the 2 strands of paste together, forming one smooth roll. Continue to roll the sausage until it is thinned to approximately 4mm (⅛in) wide. You can continue to twist the roll from either end at this stage to add more twists in the pattern.

3 Cut 6cm (2½in) lengths from the long roll and curl just the top section over to shape gently into candy canes. Leave to set for 30 minutes on non-stick paper.

4 Fill a piping bag with white royal icing, snip the end and pipe a small pearl in the centre of each candy cane. Fix the ribbon bows into position.

5 Fix the cake centrally into position on the base board and surround with the polka-dot ribbon. Trace the template on p.218 and use the pokey tool to mark the design on the cake all the way round.

6 Fit the second piping bag with the icing nozzle and fill with red royal icing. Pipe the double loop of pearls shown on p.90, and top each loop with a fleur de lys, piping the centre pearl followed by the 2 sides. Fix the candy canes into position on the top of the cake with a dab of icing.

3

4

5

6

White and Black Berries

I particularly like the stark contrast of white and dark in this cake – making it a great design for a male celebration. Any dark fruit would work – blackberries, blueberries or dark cherries. Choose a striking ribbon of a suitable width to bring the hand-moulded white and dark collars together.

You will need:
- 15cm (6in) round cake
- 15cm (6in) thick round cake board
- white chocolate plastique for the base coat and base board (see pp.71 and 72 for quantities)
- 23cm (9in) round base board
- 80cm (32in) brown grosgrain ribbon, 15mm (⅝in) wide
- royal icing, for fixing
- 200g (7oz) dark chocolate plastique
- icing sugar, for dusting
- brandy, for brushing
- 300g (10½oz) white chocolate plastique
- 55cm (22in) decorative ribbon
- 425g (14oz) blackberries

Equipment:
- small sharp scissors
- glue stick
- rolling pins, large and small
- sharp knife
- pizza wheel
- pastry brush

Preparing the cake
Place the cake on the cake board and cover with a base coat of white chocolate plastique, as shown on p.71. Line the base board with the remaining white chocolate plastique, as shown for sugar paste on p.73. Surround the base board with the brown ribbon, fixed with glue. Leave the cake and base board to dry overnight.

Decorating the cake
1 Fix the cake centrally into position on the base board, using some royal icing. Knead the dark chocolate plastique until smooth and pliable. Shape into a long sausage on a worktop lightly dusted with icing sugar, and roll out to a thickness of 3–4mm (⅛in), 60cm (24in) long and 5cm (2in) wide. Trim the long edges with a pizza wheel to leave an even collar.

2 Use a pastry brush to moisten the base of the cake all the way around with brandy. Holding the dark chocolate collar in both hands, position the collar around the base of the cake, keeping it flush with the base board. Trim the collar at the back with the knife to create a clean join.

3 Repeat step 2, using the white chocolate plastique, but this time cut only one straight edge, cutting a gentle scallop on the opposite edge instead. Switch to the smaller rolling pin and roll along the scalloped edge to thin and feather it.

4 Use a pastry brush to moisten the top half of the cake all the way around with brandy. Holding the collar in both hands, position the straight edge flush with the top of the base collar. Trim the white chocolate collar at the back with the knife to create a clean join. Use your hands to mould the collar gently at the top of the cake to create a sense of movement.

5 Fix the length of decorative ribbon around the centre of the cake to cover the join of the collars. Fill the top of the cake with the blackberries.

White Chocolate Box

Everyone needs a showstopper in their repertoire that they can pull out of the bag for a last-minute cake. This design has to beat all others. Keep a box of chocolate scrolls in the store cupboard and use them to create an impressive cake tied with a decorative ribbon and bow and filled with fresh seasonal berries. Technically, you are not creating any of the components and the cake doesn't have to be brilliantly covered to create a glorious cake that will be admired and enjoyed.

You will need:
- 15cm (6in) square cake
- 15cm (6in) thick square cake board
- white chocolate plastique, for the base coat (see p.71 for quantity)
- 23cm (9in) square silver base board
- royal icing, for fixing
- 50g (2oz) white chocolate
- 80–90 (100g/3½oz) white chocolate scrolls
- 1.2m (4ft) decorative ribbon, 25mm (1in) wide
- 600–750g (1¼–1½lb) fresh seasonal berries

Equipment:
- pastry brush
- palette knife

Preparing the cake
Place the cake on the cake board and cover with a base coat of white chocolate plastique, as shown on p.71. Place the cake centrally on the silver base board, but do not fix in place with icing.

Decorating the cake
1 Melt the white chocolate in a bowl over a pan of gently simmering water, or in the microwave. Use a pastry brush to coat one side of the cake with melted chocolate. Position the white chocolate scrolls perpendicular to the cake, keeping them straight and vertical. Continue to work your way around the entire cake.

2 Tie the decorative ribbon around the cake and finish with a bow. This not only adds decoration to the cake but also, and more importantly, holds the scrolls in position while the melted white chocolate sets.

3 Fill the chocolate box with fresh seasonal berries to the desired height. Carefully lift the cake from the silver base board with a palette knife, then transfer it to a pretty glass plate.

1

2

TIPS Chocolate scrolls usually come ready made in c.10cm (4in) lengths. Trim the cake if necessary so once covered it reaches a maximum height of 7cm (3in) to allow the fruit to sit contained inside the scrolls.

The cake can be prepared to the end of stage 2 up to 3 days in advance and filled with fresh berries just prior to serving.

Hedgerow

These cakes look adorable presented together on a white cake plate or glass stand. Perfect for a summer picnic, christening, baby shower or birthday, the cakes can be boxed if not eaten on the day for each guest to take home. The moulded flowers and insects can all be made well in advance – and if you are short on time, they can be used to decorate a batch of fairy cakes or cupcakes.

You will need (per cake):
- 5cm (2in) individual round cake (see p.69 for cutting instructions)
- 60g (2½oz) marzipan, sugar paste or white chocolate plastique, for the base coat
- 75g (3oz) white sugar paste, for the top coat
- 20cm (8in) complementary ribbon, 15mm (⅝in) wide

Plus:
- royal icing, for fixing
- bumble bees (see p.102)
- ladybirds (see p.103)
- daffodils (see p.108)
- cutter leaves (see p.104)
- poppy-style flowers (see p.107)
- buttercups (see p.109)
- plunger flowers (see p.105)

Preparing the cakes
Cover each round cake with a base coat of your choice and the sugar paste top coat, as shown on p.69. Leave to dry overnight.

Surround each cake with ribbon and fix into position with a dab of royal icing.

Decorating the cakes
Fix the components into position on the top of each cake with royal icing.

Valentine Heart

This simple design combines hand-moulded roses with hand-piped leaves to maximum effect. This cake is perfect for a romantic Valentine occasion, engagement party or wedding anniversary. Pipe a special message inside the heart for your true love.

Preparing the cake

Place the cake on the cake board and cover with a base coat of your choice, as shown on p.71, and the white sugar paste top coat, as shown on p.72. Line the base board with red sugar paste topped with edible glitter, as shown on p.73. Surround it with the 15mm (⅝in) red ribbon, fixed with glue. Leave the cake and board to dry overnight.

Fix the cake centrally into position on the base board with some royal icing and surround the cake with the 35mm (1½in) deep red satin ribbon. Wrap the wired ribbon around the cake and tie in a pretty bow at the front. Trim the tails with sharp scissors.

Decorating the cake

1 Trace the heart template on p.217 and transfer onto the top of the cake using the non-toxic pencil or the pokey tool.

2 Fill a piping bag with red royal icing, snip the end off and use to fix the red roses into position on the heart outline.

3 Fill the other piping bag with green royal icing and snip the very end as shown on p.93 for hand piping leaves. Starting at the back of the heart, pipe small leaves around the heart of roses, as shown.

You will need:

- 20cm (8in) round cake
- 20cm (8in) thick round cake board
- marzipan, sugar paste or white chocolate plastique, for the base coat (see pp.71 and 72 for quantity)
- white sugar paste, for the top coat (see p.72 for quantity)
- 30cm (12in) round base board
- red sugar paste (see p.68), for the base board (see p.72 for quantity)
- edible varnish
- red edible glitter
- 1m (39in) red ribbon, 15mm (⅝in) wide
- 1 quantity red royal icing (see pp.77–8)
- 70cm (28in) deep red satin ribbon, 35mm (1½in) wide
- 1.5m (5ft) red wired ribbon, 35mm (1½in) wide
- 30 small hand-moulded red roses (see pp.99–101), using only one centre and 2 outer petals, made the day before
- 1 quantity green royal icing (see pp.77–8)

Equipment:

- small sharp scissors
- glue stick
- tracing paper and non-toxic pencil
- pokey tool (optional)
- 2 piping bags

Rose Pearl Crown Cakes

Our elaborately decorated individual cakes have really taken off at Little Venice Cake Company. As a result of this, we decided that they needed a name befitting their status, rather than just 'cupcakes', and have named them collectively as 'crown cakes'. These crown cakes are delicately hand piped with pearls and finished with hand-piped leaves and a hand-moulded rose.

You will need (per cake):
- 5cm (2in) individual round cake (see p.69 for cutting instructions)
- 60g (2½oz) marzipan, sugar paste or white chocolate plastique, for the base coat
- 75g (3oz) white sugar paste, for the top coat
- 30g (1oz) lilac or purple sugar paste (see p.68), for the roses
- 20cm (8in) lilac or purple ribbon, 7mm (¼in) wide

Plus:
- 1 quantity white royal icing, split into 4 bowls and one coloured lilac, one deep violet, one green and one left white (see pp.77–8)

Equipment:
- small sharp scissors
- 4 piping bags
- 3 no. 1.5 icing nozzles

Preparing the cakes

Cover each round cake with a base coat of your choice and the sugar paste top coat, as shown on p.69. Leave to dry overnight.

Surround half the cakes with lilac ribbon and the other half with purple ribbon, and fix into position with a dab of royal icing. Make each hand-moulded rose, which should have 1.5cm (⅝in) diameter petals cut 3mm (⅛in) thick, using the lilac or purple sugar paste, as shown on pp.99–101.

Decorating the cakes

1 Fit 3 of the piping bags with an icing nozzle and fill with white, lilac and deep violet royal icing. Hand-pipe random pearls around each cake, concentrating the pearls towards the base and petering out as you near the top. Leave to dry for 1 hour.

2 Fill the fourth piping bag with green royal icing and snip the end to create a V, as described on p.93. Pipe 3 leaves on the top of each cake at a time.

3 Set a rose in the centre of each cake on top of the leaves.

Painting the Roses Red

What a showstopper! Tiers of chocolate truffle torte are stacked together, sandwiched with lashings of chocolate ganache buttercream. The whole cake is then coated with more ganache buttercream before being wrapped in folds of finely rolled-out chocolate plastique. This outstanding creation is then dressed with delicate chocolate fans interspersed with red-glittered, hand-moulded chocolate roses. Inspired by *Alice in Wonderland*, this cake is certainly grand enough for the Queen of Hearts!

Preparing the cake

Line the base board with chocolate plastique and spray with edible varnish (or brush with sugar glue), then dredge with some of the red edible glitter, as shown on p.73. Surround the board with 1m (39in) of the brown ribbon, fixed with glue. Leave the base board to dry overnight. Note that once the components are made, this cake is relatively quick to assemble, as the tiers are not pre-covered. For larger versions of this cake, it will be necessary to cover each tier first with chocolate plastique, then dowel and direct stack as shown on p.83. Once stacked, it can then have an additional chocolate collar to decorate.

TIP This cake, once covered and decorated, should not be refrigerated. It should be kept at room temperature, away from direct heat sources and humidity. It will keep for up to 10 days, but may begin to lose its shape over time.

You will need:

- 30cm (12in) round base board
- 2 quantities dark chocolate plastique (see p.75), for use as follows:
  ¼ quantity for covering the base board
  1 quantity to cover the cake
  ¾ quantity for 30 assorted chocolate fans
- edible varnish
- red edible glitter
- 1.7m (5ft 6in) dark brown grosgrain ribbon, 15mm (⁵⁄₈in) wide
- 20cm (8in) and 2 x 15cm (6in) single-depth chocolate truffle tortes (made using half the relevant quantities given in the recipe, see p.23)
- 1 quantity chocolate ganache buttercream (see p.53)
- 20cm (8in) thin round cake board
- icing sugar or cocoa powder, for dusting
- 20 red-glittered roses in assorted sizes (see pp.99–101), made the day before
- royal icing or melted chocolate, for fixing

Equipment:

- small sharp scissors
- glue stick
- palette knife
- rolling pin
- pizza wheel
- small rolling pin

Decorating the cake

1 Cut 1 of the 15cm (6in) cakes down to 10cm (4in) in diameter. Trim the 3 tortes as necessary to make them level, and split in half horizontally. Spread one half of each with chocolate ganache buttercream and sandwich together. Place the base tier on the thin cake board and spread the top with more buttercream.

2 Stack the middle tier directly on top of the base tier. Spread buttercream on the top of the second tier and place the top tier into position. The middle and top tiers will not require their own cake boards, and the cake will not need to be dowelled as these are only single depths and, overall, it is quite a small cake.

3 Using a palette knife, start covering the sides and visible tops of the tiers with buttercream.

4 Continue until everything is covered with a thin layer of buttercream. The finish does not need to be smooth, as all the buttercream will be covered.

5 Divide the chocolate plastique for covering the cake into 3, and knead the first part until smooth and pliable but not soft. Roll into a sausage and place on a worktop lightly dusted with icing sugar or cocoa powder. Press diagonally along the chocolate plastique in both directions with a rolling pin to flatten it slightly. This encourages the sausage to retain its shape as it is rolled. Continue to roll out the collar to a thickness of 3mm (¹⁄₈in). The width should be 10–15cm (4–6in) and the length close to 75cm (30in).

6 Using a pizza wheel, as this will not stretch or tear the chocolate plastique, trim one long edge so it is straight.

7 Hold the pizza wheel on the opposite long edge and draw it along in waves to create a scalloped edge.

8 Roll a small rolling pin, held just across the scalloped edge, to thin, feather and texture the waves, pressing just lightly.

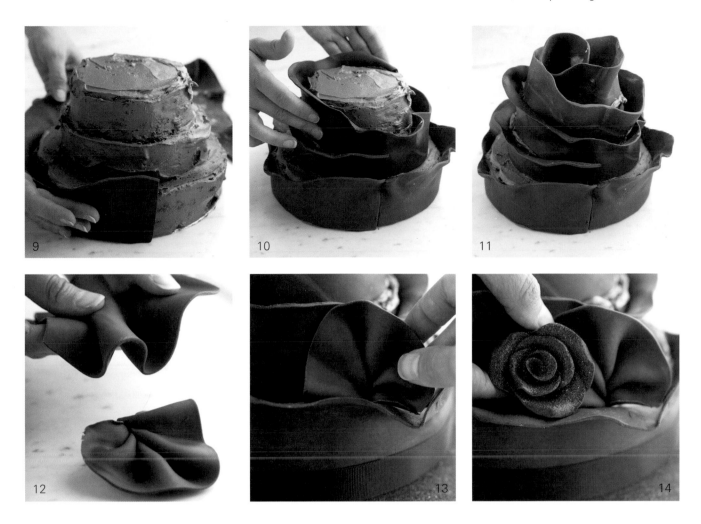

9 Lift the prepared chocolate collar carefully and wrap it around the base tier, ensuring the straight edge is flush with the base of the cake. Trim with a sharp knife so the collar joins neatly at the back of the cake.

10 Repeat, using the remaining chocolate plastique, to make 2 further collars of the same size for the remaining tiers. Fit the first one in place, working your way up the cake a little more.

11 Add the last collar, working your way up to the top and finishing with a flourish on the top tier.

12 Roll out the chocolate plastique for the fans and trim with the pizza wheel to rectangles measuring roughly 10 x 15cm (4 x 6in). Working quickly, so that you keep the chocolate plastique soft and pliable, fold each rectangle to make a fan and pinch the 2 shorter ends together at the base to finish.

13 Carefully place the cake in position on the base board, held in place with a dab of royal icing or melted chocolate. Surround the bottom tier with the remaining ribbon and fix with glue. Starting with the base tier, place a freshly made chocolate fan inside the collar, adhering it to the chocolate ganache buttercream on the cake.

14 Now fix the first glitter rose in place, nestled up to the fan and facing outwards. Repeat until the entire cake is dressed with fans and roses, teasing the fans into position to frame the roses, fillling the gaps and blending all the elements well with the collar.

Chocolate Glitter Roses

Chocolate and gold have a rich affinity for premium indulgence. These crown cakes look stunning presented together at a festive party. I like to use chocolate cake, but filled with different buttercreams – vanilla, white chocolate and coffee being my favourites.

You will need (per cake):
- 4cm (1¹/₂in) individual square cake (see p.66 for cutting instructions)
- 60g (2¹/₂oz) marzipan, sugar paste or white chocolate plastique, for the base coat
- 75g (3oz) dark chocolate plastique, for the top coat
- 20cm (8in) dark brown grosgrain ribbon, 15mm (⁵/₈in) wide
- 30cm (12in) gold ribbon, 7mm (³/₈in) wide
- hand-moulded, gold-glittered, dark chocolate roses (see pp.99–101)

Plus:
- melted dark chocolate, for fixing

Equipment:
- small sharp scissors

Preparing the cakes
Cover each cake with a base coat of your choice, as shown on pp.66–7, and the top coat, as shown on p.68. Leave to dry overnight.

Surround the cakes with the dark brown ribbon and fix in place with a dab of melted chocolate. Place the thinner gold ribbon over the brown ribbon, tie in a double knot and trim the ends with sharp scissors.

Decorating the cakes
Fix a gold-glittered dark chocolate rose into position on the top of each cake with melted dark chocolate.

Shoe Couture

A girl can never have too many shoes, so fill a shoebox with your favourite designs! We design a new collection of cakes every season for the London store Harvey Nichols. These delicate shoes are intricate and will require patience and a steady hand. Make several pairs at a time, as they do keep well.

Preparing the cakes

Cover each cake with a base coat of your choice and the white sugar paste top coat, as shown on p.69. Leave to dry overnight.

Surround the cakes with double layers of ribbons, fixed in place with a dab of royal icing.

TIP If glittering any of the shoes, brush each pair with sugar glue, then dip into a bowl of glitter. Remove and shake off the excess before icing the shoes into place.

Decorating the cakes

1 Trace the shoe template on p.218 onto a thin piece of plastic or stiff card and cut out with a scalpel. Knead the tan and black petal pastes until smooth and pliable, then roll them on a sugar-dusted worktop to a thickness of just 2mm (¹⁄₈in). Cut out 2 templates for each pair of shoes: half tan, the other half black.

2 Stack the 2 square cake boards with the smaller one centrally on top. Place the shoe soles around the edge of the cake boards as shown, shaping the soles so that the heel is on the top board and the toe on the base board. Roll a long, thin strand each of tan and black petal paste to make the heels, and cut with a sharp knife into 8–10mm (around ³⁄₈in) lengths. Leave to dry for 1 hour.

3 To pipe the toes, fit 2 of the piping bags with a no. 3 nozzle and fill one with peach and one with black royal icing. Using the black icing, pressure-pipe the toe of each of the black soles to fill the front of the shoe. This can then be overpiped with a bow piped from a piping bag fitted with a no. 1.5 nozzle and filled with red icing, decorated with a round glittered pearl (or use a silver dragee sugar decoration) or left plain. Repeat, building up the toes, using the tan royal icing on the tan soles.

4 Build up the back of each tan-soled shoe, using the remaining peach icing in a bag fitted with a no. 1.5 nozzle, and the remaining black icing for each black-soled shoe, in another bag with the same-size nozzle. Pipe along the outline of the shoe from one side of the toe to the other, letting the icing fall into position. Pipe a second line over the first, starting and finishing a little way back. Repeat with a third and fourth line, starting each a little further back. Leave for 1 hour.

5 Turn the shoes on their side and ice the heels into position. Leave for 1 hour, then ice into position.

Florence Cupcake

This adorable Florence cupcake would grace any little girl's birthday party or christening. The cake features a threaded effect of ribbon and bows, with a hand-moulded teddy bear holding a sugar cupcake, and sitting amongst more cupcakes and some pretty flowers.

You will need:
- 15cm (6in) round cake
- marzipan, sugar paste or white chocolate plastique, for the base coat (see p.71 for quantity)
- ivory sugar paste (see p.68) , for the top coat and the base board (see p.72 for quantities)
- 70cm (28in) rose geranium ribbon, 25mm (1in) wide
- royal icing, for fixing
- 23cm (9in) round base board
- 95cm (38in) rose geranium ribbon, 15mm (5/8in) wide
- 3m (10ft) rose geranium ribbon, 3mm (1/8in) wide
- 160g (6oz) petal paste, coloured (see p.68) as follows:
  65g (2¼oz) light brown
  20g (¾oz) ivory
  40g (1½oz) rose geranium pink
  25g (1oz) dark brown
  5g (¼oz) white
  5g (¼oz) black
- icing sugar, for dusting
- stick of spaghetti
- sugar glue
- sugar sprinkles
- 6 small pink plunger flowers (see p.105)

Equipment:
- sharp scissors
- glue stick
- tracing paper and fine-liner pen
- pokey tool
- ribbon insertion tools
- small rolling pin
- 7.5cm (3in) frill cutter
- frilling tool
- 2.5cm (1in) round cutter
- sharp knife
- smiley tool

Preparing the cake

Place the cake on the cake board and cover with a base coat of your choice, as shown on p.71, and the ivory sugar paste top coat, as shown on p.72. Surround the cake with the 25mm (1in) rose geranium ribbon and fix with a dab of royal icing. Line the base board with the remaining ivory sugar paste, as shown on p.73, and surround with the 15mm (5/8in) ivory ribbon, fixed with glue. Leave the cake and board to dry overnight.

Decorating the cake

Fix the cake centrally into position on the base board with royal icing. Trace the template on p.216 and transfer onto the cake above the ribbon, using the pokey tool. Insert the 3mm (1/8in) rose geranium ribbon as shown on p.111, using the ribbon insertion tools. Use the remainder of the ribbon to make 12 ribbon bows, as shown on p.110, and use to top each ribbon loop swag.

Using the different petal pastes, make the bear components as follows:

light brown: shaped into a body, head, arms, paws, ears and muzzle; use the large and small ball tools to indent the details on the paws.

ivory: shaped to make the frosting for the 5 tiny sugar cupcakes.

pink: shaped into pieces for the skirt bow, and the rest kneaded until it is malleable, then rolled out on a worktop lightly dusted with icing sugar to a depth of 2–3mm (1/8in) and a 7.5cm (3in) frill cut out with the frill cutter

dark brown: some moulded into a small triangle for the nose; the rest reserved for the cupcakes

white: shaped into 2 eyes

black: shaped into 2 pupils

1 Use the frilling tool positioned 2.5cm (1in) within the scalloped edge and frill the edge all the way around. You may find it helpful to frill on a foam pad (see p.107).

2 Use the round cutter in the centre of the frill to remove the centre.

3 Cut the frill with a sharp knife.

4 Insert a 5cm (2in) piece of the spaghetti into the bear's body. Paint a little sugar glue around the middle of the bear's body, place the frilled skirt over the teddy bear and press into position.

5 Position the bear's arms and paws and fix into position with sugar glue. (Note that the hind paws attach straight to the body.)

6 Spear the teddy bear's head on the spaghetti and fix with sugar glue.

7 Glue the muzzle into position, indent the smile with the smiley tool and poke both ends of the smile with the pokey tool. Glue the nose into position.

8 Glue the ears into position and add the white and then black circles for the eyes. Fix one of the small flowers next to one of the ears.

9 Make the ribbon bow for the back of the skirt and fix into position with sugar glue.

10 To make the cupcakes, shape each base in the remaining dark brown petal paste and mark vertical lines with the pokey tool. Glue the ivory sugar paste for the frosting into position and brush with sugar glue. Roll the top of each cake in a small bowl of sugar sprinkles and leave to set. Insert a 3cm (1¼in) length of spaghetti directly into the teddy's tummy between her arm paws, protruding outwards by 1cm (³⁄₈in). Slide one of the cupcakes onto the spaghetti, using sugar glue to fix.

Use the remaining sugar cupcakes and small pink flowers to dress the cake, fixing them into position with royal icing. Finally, carefully transfer the teddy bear to the cake with a palette knife and fix in place with some royal icing.

Pirate Treasure

Aye aye, Captain. This is the perfect cake for all our hero pirates, and one on which to test your hand-moulding skills. Young boys will love this cake, complete with pirate, Pretty Polly parrot, treasure chest and 'X marks the spot' map.

You will need:

- 15cm (6in) square cake
- 15cm (6in) thick square cake board
- marzipan, sugar paste or white chocolate plastique, for the base coat (see pp.71 and 72 for quantity)
- white sugar paste, for the top coat (see p.72 for quantity)
- 70cm (28in) blue ribbon, 25mm (1in) wide
- 1 quantity each black and gold royal icing (see pp.77–8)
- 23cm (9in) square base board
- blue sugar paste (see p.68), for the base board (see p.72 for quantity)
- blue edible glitter
- 95cm (38in) blue ribbon, 15mm (5⁄8in) wide
- 100g (3½oz) gold sugar paste (see p.68)
- 40g (1½oz) golden caster sugar
- 200g (7¼oz) petal paste, coloured as follows: 50g (2oz) black, 40g (1½oz) white, 40g (1½oz) pale pink/peach, 40g (1½oz) dark brown, 10g (¼oz) green, 10g (¼oz) gold, 5g (⅛oz) orange and 5g (⅛oz) yellow
- ½ tsp gold lustre
- 1 tsp dipping alcohol
- 5cm (2in) stick of spaghetti

Equipment:

- sharp scissors
- glue stick
- small rolling pin
- sharp knife
- sugar glue
- pastry brushes
- ball tool
- foam pad
- 2 piping bags
- no. 1.5 and no. 2 icing nozzles
- pokey tool
- paintbrush
- smiley tool

Preparing the cake

Place the cake on the cake board and cover with a base coat of your choice, as shown on p.71, and the white sugar paste top coat, as shown on p.72. Surround the cake with the 25mm (1in) blue ribbon, fixed in place with a dab of royal icing.

Line the base board with blue sugar paste topped with glitter, as shown on p.73. Fix the cake centrally into position on the base board with royal icing and surround the board with the 15mm (5⁄8in) blue ribbon, fixed with glue. Leave the cake and base board to dry overnight.

Decorating the cake

1 Roll out the gold sugar paste to a thickness of 3mm (1⁄8in) and trim the edges with a sharp knife to a wavy 'island' shape design. Brush the top of the icing with sugar glue, using a pastry brush, and sprinkle with the sugar.

2 Brush the top of the cake with a little water, using a pastry brush, and lay the dusted sugar-paste island over the cake off centre.

4

5

3 For the map, roll out a piece of the pale pink/peach paste until it is wafer thin, then frill the edges with a ball tool on a foam pad (see p.107). Leave to dry for 30 minutes. Fit a piping bag with the no. 1.5 nozzle and fill with black royal icing. Pipe the map details, then leave to set for 1 hour.

4 Make the treasure chest using the dark brown petal paste (reserving enough for the pirate's hair) by shaping a base, approximately 4 x 2.5cm (1½ x 1in), a lid and a roll of paste to hold the chest lid open, as shown. Roll thin strips of the gold petal paste and make 2 straps, and also a lock by pressing a pokey tool into a flattened circle of paste. Use sugar glue to fix these elements into place.

5 Fit the second piping bag with the no. 2 nozzle and fill with gold royal icing. Pipe small coin shapes inside the chest, and continue to build up different layers of piped coins. Leave to set for 2 hours. Blend the gold lustre and dipping alcohol together and brush over the coins, straps and lock with a paintbrush.

3

6 To make the pirate, create the shapes as shown: body, shoulders and eye in white; legs, feet, hat, eye and eyepatch in black; head, arms, ears and nose in skin colour; and curls of hair in dark brown made by rolling 5 pea-sized balls into rounded cones.

 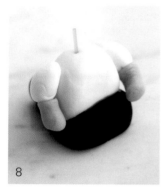  

7 Fix the body into position on the legs. Use sugar glue to fix the components together. Bend the legs backwards so the pirate is kneeling, and add the feet.

8 Thread the spaghetti through the body and legs to support the head. Glue the arms into position and indent the ball tool at the end.

9 Fix the head into position and use the smiley tool to add the smile.

10 Add the nose and one eye.

11 Glue the small black eye patch into position. Pinch the 4 corners of the square hat together to create a pirate hat and shape over the pirate's head.

12 Fix the pirate's hair into position, protruding from under his hat. Add the ears.

13 Use the piping bag of black icing to pipe 2 strands to resemble the string on either side of the eye patch.

14 Assemble the parrot from its component parts of green body, wings and tail and orange beak. Cut the piece of yellow paste into the bird's crest with a sharp knife and attach to the head. Fix the parrot into position on the pirate's shoulder and pipe 2 black eyes with the black royal icing.

15 Fix all the components into position on the top of the cake.

Penguin Pudding

How cute is this Christmas cake? Our cheeky penguin, standing with his chef's hat and wooden spoon, is hand moulded. The cake has been baked in a pudding mould and then covered with chocolate plastique and finished with cut-out holly leaves and glitter berries. Guaranteed to fill you with festive cheer!

You will need:

- 15cm (6in) quantity of chocolate truffle torte recipe (see p.22) cooked in a 450ml (1 pint) pudding basin, 14cm (5½in) in diameter
- 1 quantity dark chocolate plastique (see p.75)
- 23cm (9in) round base board
- red sugar paste (see p.68), for the base board (see p.72 for quantity)
- edible varnish or sugar glue
- red edible glitter
- 80cm (32in) red ribbon, 15mm (⅜in) wide
- 100g (3½oz) white sugar paste
- icing sugar, for dusting
- 75g (3oz) green sugar paste (see p.68)
- 50g (2oz) red sugar paste
- royal icing, for fixing
- cutter white snowflakes (see p.189), optional

For the penguin:

- 20g (¾oz) light brown petal paste
- 80g (3oz) white petal paste
- 80g (3oz) white sugar paste
- food colourings in black and orange
- stick of spaghetti, broken to give a 6cm (2½in) piece and a 3cm (1¼in) piece

Equipment:

- paintbrush (optional)
- glue stick
- small rolling pin
- 8cm (3¼in) holly cutter
- marking tool
- sharp knife
- pastry brush
- 3.5cm (1½in) round cutter

Preparing the cake

Cover the cake with one coat of dark chocolate plastique, as shown on p.71. Line the base board with red sugar paste topped with glitter, as shown on p.73 (reserving some for the holly berries). Surround the base board with the red ribbon, fixed with glue. Leave the cake and base board to dry overnight.

Knead the white sugar paste until smooth and pliable and roll out on a worktop dusted with icing sugar to approximately a 20cm (8in) circle, 3mm (⅛in) thick. Cut a scalloped edge all the way around. Brush the top of the cake with cooled boiled water and place the white sugar paste into position over the top of the cake.

Decorating the cake

1 Knead the green sugar paste until smooth and pliable and roll out to a thickness of 3mm (⅛in). Cut out 3 holly leaves, using the holly-leaf cutter.

1.

2

3

2 Mark the indentations on the leaves with a marking tool or use a sharp knife gently. Brush the underside of the leaves with sugar glue, then fix into position on the top of the pudding as shown.

3 Roll 6 pea-sized balls of red sugar paste and place in a small dish of the reserved red glitter to cover. Use royal icing to fix these into position on the top of the holly leaves.

4 To make the penguin, first shape the wooden spoon from the light brown petal paste, then leave it to set hard. Next, knead the white petal and white sugar pastes together thoroughly, then divide into 3 portions, weighing 90g (3½oz), 40g (1½oz) and 30g (1oz). Colour the largest portion black and the smallest portion orange, and leave the middle one white. Now mould the different-coloured pastes into the body parts, as shown: head, body, flippers and eyes in black; beak and feet in orange; hat, eyes and tummy (using the round cutter) in white.

5 Place the orange feet together and brush the back of them with a little sugar glue. Press the body down onto the feet to secure. Brush the body with sugar glue and fix the white tummy into position. Insert the 6cm (2½in) length of spaghetti into the body.

6 Fix the penguin's flippers into position from the back of the body, making sure that the flippers are folded gently outwards from the body.

7 Fix the head into position on top of the spaghetti. Fix the eyes and beak into position with sugar glue.

8 Insert a 3cm (1¼in) length of spaghetti into the top of the penguin's head and fix the chef's hat into position with sugar glue. Finish by inserting the wooden spoon into the penguin's body so it sits by his flipper, as shown. Fix the cake into position offset on the base board with royal icing, and fix the penguin in position at the front. Add some white snowflakes, if using.

TIP If you don't have a holly-leaf cutter, you can cut these leaves out with a small knife freehand, or make a template from card.

Crown Glitter Hearts

These cakes use the simplest technique, yet are so effective. They are guaranteed to be eye-catching, presented *en masse* at a birthday party or presented as a group of four or nine in a presentation box. Change the organza ribbon to complement the colour of the party – or colour code them for the boys and girls.

Preparing the cakes

Cover each cake with a base coat of your choice, as shown on pp.66–7, and the sugar paste top coat, as shown on pp.68. Leave to dry overnight.

Surround the cakes with the organza ribbon and tie in a bow, trimming the ends neatly with the sharp scissors.

Decorating the cakes

1 Knead the grey sugar paste until pliable but not sticky, and roll out on a clean work surface, dusted with icing sugar, to a thickness of 4mm (¼in). Stamp heart shapes out using the cutter and place on non-stick paper.

2 Spray the hearts with edible varnish or brush with sugar glue, then dredge with silver glitter. Leave to set before carefully removing each heart to a clean cake board to firm up, which takes 1 hour.

3 Fill a piping bag with white royal icing and snip the end. Pipe a pearl in the centre of each cake and place a silver glitter heart into position.

You will need (per cake):

- 4cm (1½in) individual square cake (see p.66 for cutting instructions)
- 60g (2½oz) marzipan, sugar paste or white chocolate plastique, for the base coat
- 75g (3oz) white sugar paste, for the top coat
- 35cm (14in) organza ribbon, 15mm (⅝in) wide

Plus:

- 1 quantity grey sugar paste (see p.68)
- icing sugar, for dusting
- edible varnish or sugar glue
- silver edible glitter
- royal icing, for fixing

Equipment:

- small sharp scissors
- rolling pin
- 3.5cm (1½in) heart cutter
- sheet of non-stick paper
- paintbrush (optional)
- cake board
- piping bag

Daffodil Easter Cake

This clever design has maximum impact for an Easter or spring celebration. I have baked the cake in a silicone bundt mould, which creates the detailed pattern and texture on the cake. It is then frosted with lemon glacé icing and decorated with sugar daffodils, plunger flowers and tiny ladybirds. This is a great cake to prepare ahead and make with children.

Preparing the cake

Lie a sheet of non-stick baking parchment under a wire rack, and place the cake on the rack. Spoon the glacé icing over the cake.

Decorating the cake

Place the first daffodil into position, then build up the decoration as you work around the ring, adding plunger flowers and moulded ladybirds. The decorations will adhere to the icing

Leave the icing to set, then place the cake on a pretty plate.

You will need:

- 20cm (8in) quantity of any of the cake recipes (see pp.18–45), baked in a 20cm (8in) silicone bundt mould
- ½ quantity lemon glacé icing (see p.58)
- 3 hand-moulded ladybirds (see p.103)
- 6 cutter daffodils (see p.108)
- plunger flowers (see p.105) in white, yellow and lilac, made with the following size cutters: 4mm (¼in), 7mm (⅓in) and 10mm (⅜in)

Snowflake

This is a stylish design for a classic Christmas cake. The combination of regal purple, crisp white and silver glitter combines well to create this striking cake. The snowflakes, which are made with cutters, trail down onto the purple-iced base board, and the cake and board are finished with simple iced purple and white pearls.

You will need:

- 15cm (6in) round cake
- 15cm (6in) thick round cake board
- marzipan, sugar paste or white chocolate plastique, for the base coat (see pp.71 and 72 for quantity)
- white sugar paste, for the top coat (see p.72 for quantity), plus 75g (3oz) for the snowflakes
- 75g (3oz) grey sugar paste (see p.68)
- 23cm (9in) round base board
- purple sugar paste (see p.68), for the base board (see p.72 for quantity), plus 75g (3oz) for the snowflakes
- 80cm (32in) purple ribbon, 15mm (5/8in) wide
- 55cm (22in) purple ribbon, 25mm (1in) wide
- 1 quantity white royal icing (see p.77)
- icing sugar, for dusting
- edible varnish or sugar glue
- silver edible glitter
- white hologram glitter
- 1 quantity purple royal icing (see pp.77–8)

Equipment:

- glue stick
- small rolling pin
- plunger snowflake cutters: small (2cm/3/4in), medium (3cm/11/4in) and large (4cm/13/4in)
- non-stick baking parchment
- paintbrush (optional)
- 2 piping bags
- 2 no. 2 icing nozzles

Preparing the cake

Place the cake on the cake board and cover with a base coat of your choice, as shown on p.71, and the white sugar paste top coat, as shown on p.72. Line the base board with purple sugar paste, as shown on p.73. Surround the base board with the 15mm (5/8in) ribbon, fixed with glue, and surround the cake with the 25mm (1in) ribbon, fixed with a dab of royal icing. Leave the cake and base board to dry overnight.

Decorating the cake

1 Fix the cake into position offset on the base board. To make the snowflakes, take the extra purple sugar paste and knead until smooth and pliable. Roll out to a thickness of 3mm (1/8in) on a worktop lightly dusted with icing sugar. Use the plunger snowflake cutters to stamp out and indent 3 snowflakes of each size, then set aside on non-stick baking parchment dusted with icing sugar to firm. Repeat with the extra white and the grey sugar paste.

2 To glitter, place a selection of snowflakes on a sheet of non-stick baking parchment and spray with edible varnish or brush with sugar glue. Sprinkle with some of the silver or white glitter. (They don't have to be fully dredged – more just sparkling!) Glitter the white, grey and purple snowflakes separately. Leave to firm for about 2 hours or overnight.

3 Fit both piping bags with icing nozzles; fill one with white royal icing and the other with purple royal icing. Fix the snowflakes into position with corresponding colours of royal icing, starting on the top of the cake and working down over the side and onto the base board. They can overlap a bit.

4 To finish, hand pipe pearls in white and purple between and around the snowflakes, as shown on p.90.

1

2

3

4

Crowning Glory

These simple, yet stunning, plain cakes, with their golden crowns, were part of a range we launched at Harvey Nichols. (Instructions for the candy-striped cakes and their roses, shown interspersed here, can be found on pp.91 and 99.) You could change the mood by using the heart cutter for Valentine's Day, or perhaps bells for a wedding.

Preparing the cakes

Cover each cake with a base coat of your choice and the white sugar paste top coat, as shown on p.69. Leave to dry overnight.

Decorating the cakes

1 To make each crown, roll out the gold sugar paste to a depth of 3mm (1/8in), then stamp out a heart with the cutter.

2 Roll a strand of paste to 3mm (1/8in) thick and wind this around the top section of the crown.

3 Trim with a sharp knife and cut off the pointed base. Roll and cut a piece of paste with tapered sides for the base of the crown. Use sugar glue to fix this into position.

4 Add another piece of paste to build up the shape of the crown, again attaching it with sugar glue.

5 Fit the piping bag with the no. 2 nozzle and fill with gold royal icing. Hand pipe pearls and jewels onto the crown.

6 Pipe 2 fleurs de lys onto the crown, and then pipe a larger fleur de lys on the top (see main picture). Leave to dry for 1 hour. Mix some gold lustre and dipping alcohol on a 1:2 ratio, then brush over the decoration. Fix each crown into position on a cake with a dab of royal icing.

You will need (per cake):
- 5cm (2in) individual round cake (see p.69 for cutting instructions)
- 60g (2½oz) marzipan, sugar paste or white chocolate plastique, for the base coat
- 75g (3oz) white sugar paste, for the top coat
- 20cm (8in) red ribbon, 15mm (5/8in) wide
- 20cm (8in) blue ribbon, 7mm (5/16in) wide
- 20g (3/4oz) gold sugar paste (see p.68)

Plus:
- 1 quantity gold royal icing (see pp.77–8)
- sugar glue
- gold lustre
- dipping alcohol

Equipment:
- small sharp scissors
- piping bag
- no. 2 icing nozzle
- 3cm (1¼in) heart cutter
- sharp knife
- paintbrush

1

2

3

4

5

6

Frilly Citrus Roses

These tangerine and lime roses work well on plain white-iced cakes. The roses are frilled and shaped before being dusted, to create shading and texture. The centres have been made by rolling a ball of petal paste in a dish of caster sugar mixed with colour dust. Made entirely in white, these would look stunning at a summer wedding.

You will need (per cake):
- 5cm (2in) individual round cake (see p.69 for cutting instructions)
- 60g (2½oz) marzipan, sugar paste or white chocolate plastique, for the base coat
- 75g (3oz) white sugar paste, for the top coat
- 20cm (8in) green or orange ribbon, 15mm (⅝in) wide

Plus:
- royal icing, for fixing
- orange and green petal paste, for the roses (use the poppy method on p.107)
- 2 tsp each orange and green colour dusts
- dipping alcohol
- sugar glue
- 2 tbsp caster sugar

Equipment:
- small sharp scissors
- piping bag
- paint palette
- paintbrush

Preparing the cakes
Cover each cake with a base coat of your choice and the sugar paste top coat, as shown on p.69. Leave to dry overnight. Surround half the cakes with green ribbon and the other half with orange ribbon, and fix into position with a dab of royal icing.

Decorating the cakes
1 Cut out the roses from the petal paste (half in green, half in orange), and place the top layer of petals of each rose into a paint palette to dry, so that they set in a curled shape.

2 Blend together 1 teaspoon of each colour dust with a little dipping alcohol (a) and brush each row of petals with colour to build up the intensity (b). Fix the layers of petals together with sugar glue.

3 In a small dish, stir together half the caster sugar with the remaining green colour dust. Roll a coloured ball of petal paste to the size of a small pea and brush with sugar glue before rolling it in the sugar to cover (c).

4 Fix the green petal paste ball in the centre of a green rose with a dab of royal icing. Repeat to make enough green centres for half the roses, then make a similar number of orange centres.

5 Fix the flowers on top of each cake with royal icing.

a

b

c

Flower Power

Bright and modern, this cake combines the use of cutters with hand piping. A simple yet impactful design means that you can change the colours of the découpage flowers to complement your celebration. The tiers can be made from different recipes, with additional crown cakes made and decorated with a funky flower for guests to take home. For a more masculine version, use different-sized circles or stars, rather than flowers.

1

2

3

Preparing the cakes

Place the cakes on cake boards of the same size and cover with a base coat of your choice, as shown on p.71, and the white sugar paste top coat, as shown on p.72. Line the base board with white sugar paste, as shown on p.73. Surround the base board and both tiers with the aqua ribbon, fixed with glue and royal icing respectively. Leave the cakes and base board to dry overnight.

Fix the base tier centrally into position on the base board, using some of the royal icing. To assemble, prepare the base tier for stacking, and fix the top tier into position, offset to one side.

Decorating the cakes

1 To make the découpage flowers, knead the coloured sugar pastes separately until smooth and pliable. Roll out the colour for a large base flower first, to a depth of 3mm (⅛in), on a worktop dusted with icing sugar. Cut out a flower with the large cutter. Then cut out a middle-sized flower in a second colour and the smallest flower in a third colour. Repeat, using different combinations of sizes and colours, so you have got a good selection of flowers to work with.

2 Brush a little sugar glue onto the cake and fix the first base flower into position. Brush the centre of this flower with sugar glue and fix a middle flower in place, followed by more glue and a small flower, to build up the design. Repeat randomly over the cake, using the different flowers of different sizes and colours. Work quickly to avoid the sugar paste drying out.

3 Fit the piping bag with the icing nozzle and fill with the yellow royal icing. Hand pipe pearls directly on to the petals and between the flowers, to finish.

You will need:

- 10cm (4in) and 20cm (8in) round cakes
- 10cm (4in) and 20cm (8in) thick round cake boards
- marzipan, sugar paste or white chocolate plastique, for the base coat (see pp.71 and 72 for quantities)
- white sugar paste, for the top coat and base board (see p.72 for quantities)
- 30cm (12in) round base board
- 2.1m (7ft) aqua ribbon, 15mm (⅝in) wide
- 1 quantity yellow royal icing (see pp.77–8)
- 100g (3½oz) each sugar paste in aqua, orange and yellow (see p.68)
- 5-petal flower cutters: small (2.5cm/1in), medium (5cm/2in) and large (7.5cm/3in)
- 6 dowelling rods
- sugar glue

Equipment:

- glue stick
- piping bag
- no. 2 icing nozzle

Honeybees

These hand-painted honeybee cakes were commissioned exclusively for Fortnum & Mason, as they keep hives to make their own honey on the roof of their famous building in London's Piccadilly. To show off the detail and the wings, I have chosen a strong eau de nil background colour to cover the cakes.

1

2

3

You will need (per cake):

- 5cm (2in) individual round cake (see p.69 for cutting instructions)
- 60g (2½oz) marzipan, sugar paste or white chocolate plastique, for the base coat
- 75g (3oz) eau de nil sugar paste (see p.68), for the top coat
- 20cm (8in) eau de nil ribbon, 15mm (⅝in) wide

Plus:

- 1 quantity royal icing (see p.77)
- cocoa butter
- white, yellow and black colour dusts

Equipment:

- small sharp scissors
- tracing paper and fine-liner pen
- non-toxic pencil
- piping bag
- no. 1.5 icing nozzle
- medium and fine paintbrushes

Preparing the cakes

Cover each cake with a base coat of your choice and the sugar paste top coat, as shown on p.69. Leave to dry overnight. Surround each cake with ribbon and fix into position with a dab of royal icing.

Decorating the cakes

1 Trace the honeybee template on p.212 and transfer it 4 times onto each cake – 3 times clustered on the top and once on the side. Place the cocoa butter in a saucer over a pan of simmering water and add little piles of each of the colour dusts around the edge.

2 Once the cocoa butter has melted, use the medium paintbrush to blend a little of it with the white colour dust, then paint the honeybees' wings. Similarly, blend the other colours and paint the bodies and heads yellow (then allow to set for 20 minutes). Finally, paint black stripes over the bodies and add the black detail with a fine paintbrush.

3 Fit the piping bag with the nozzle and fill with the royal icing. Hand-pipe delicate white pearls between the honeybees. Leave to dry for 1 hour.

Passion Flower

An impressive botanical cake, this design involves hand-painting passion flowers and buds over two tiers. It is elegant and detailed, and so I have purposely not added any further decoration, preferring to let guests appreciate the intricacies of the painting.

Preparing the cake

Place the cake on the cake board and cover with a base coat of your choice, as shown on pp.71, and the buttermilk sugar paste top coat, as shown on p.72. Line the base board with buttermilk sugar paste, as shown on p.73. Surround the base board and both tiers with the green ribbon, fixed with glue and a dab of royal icing respectively. Leave the cakes and base board to dry overnight.

Decorating the cake

1 Fix the base tier centrally into position on the base board with some royal icing. Prepare the base tier for stacking, as shown on p.83. Trace the template on p.215 and transfer the design onto the 2 tiers.

2 Prepare a saucer of colour dusts and cocoa butter over a saucepan of simmering water, and mix the colours as required. Begin painting the base colours of the passion flowers, building up the layers.

3 Add more detail to the flowers and paint the stalks and leaves. Finish with the deeper purple strokes of the passion flower. Leave to set for 2 hours.

4 To assemble, fix the top tier into position.

You will need:

- 10cm (4in) and 20cm (8in) round cakes
- 10cm (4in) and 20cm (8in) thick round cake boards
- marzipan, sugar paste or white chocolate plastique, for the base coat (see p.71 for quantities)
- buttermilk sugar paste (see p.68), for the top coat and base board (see p.72 for quantities)
- 30cm (12in) round base board
- 1.7m (5ft 8in) sage green grosgrain ribbon, 15mm (⅝in) wide
- royal icing, for fixing
- 6 dowelling rods
- colour dusts in ivory, white, lilac, purple and greens
- cocoa butter

Equipment:

- glue stick
- assorted paintbrushes
- tracing paper and fine-liner pen
- non-toxic pencil

Rose Couture

This cake was inspired by an Oscar de la Renta gown with a gorgeous nipped-in waist and a full skirt adorned with bold, bright red blooms. I chose to paint the blooms on this four-tier wedding cake and blocked the base tier with open roses and ribbon loops. Changing the colours will dramatically alter this cake to make it bespoke for any wedding.

You will need:

- 10cm (4in), 15cm (6in) (cut to 5cm/2in deep), 20cm (8in) and 25cm (10in) round cakes
- 10cm (4in), 15cm (6in), 20cm (8in) and 25cm (10in) thick round cake boards
- marzipan, sugar paste or white chocolate plastique, for the base coat (see pp.71 and 72 for quantity)
- white sugar paste, for the top coat and base board (see p.72 for quantities)
- 2.5m (8ft 3in) red ribbon, 15mm (⁵/₈in) wide
- 2.5m (8ft 3in) black ribbon, 9mm (³/₈in) wide
- 1 quantity red royal icing (see pp.77–8)
- 33cm (13in) round base board
- 1.1m (3ft 8in) black ribbon, 15mm (⁵/₈in) wide
- 18 dowelling rods
- 15cm (6in) round polystyrene block, 5cm (2in) deep
- 12in (30cm) red ribbon, 25mm (1in) wide
- cocoa butter
- red, black, white and burgundy colour dusts
- 250g (9oz) red sugar paste (see p.68)
- open roses: 6 red, 6 orange and 6 yellow (see p.106)
- triple ribbon loops with tails (see pp.112–13), as follows.

  10 black loops using 8m (26ft) ribbon, 9mm (³/₈in) wide

  10 red loops using 8m (26ft) ribbon, 15mm (⁵/₈in) wide

  10 red organza loops using 8m (26ft) ribbon, 25mm (1in) wide

Equipment:

- small sharp scissors
- stick glue
- tracing paper and fine-liner pen
- non-toxic pencil (optional)
- pokey tool
- 4–5 assorted paintbrushes
- piping bag

Preparing the cake

Place the cakes on the cake boards of the same size and cover with a base coat of your choice, as shown on p.71, and the white sugar paste top coat, as shown on p.72. Surround all the cakes with the 15mm (⁵/₈in) red ribbon overlaid with the 9mm (³/₈in) black ribbon, fixed in place with a dab of royal icing. Line the base board with white sugar paste, as shown on p.73, and surround it with the 15mm (⁵/₈in) black ribbon, fixed with stick glue. Leave the cakes and base board to dry overnight.

Prepare the top 3 tiers for direct stacking, as shown on p.83. Surround the polystyrene block with the 25mm (1in) red ribbon and fix with the glue stick. Fix the base tier centrally into position on the base board with a dab of royal icing, and prepare the base tier to be blocked, as shown on p.82, using the polystyrene block. Add some royal icing to the top of this block and fix the top 3 stacked tiers into position.

Decorating the cake

Trace the template of the rose on p.214 and transfer it onto the entire cake with the pokey tool, or draw freehand with a non-toxic pencil, thinking about the layout and positioning to build up your design (see p.115). You can always add more roses once you start painting. Prepare a saucer of colour dusts and cocoa butter over a saucepan of simmering water, and mix the colours as required. Paint the design in stages, starting with the background and gradually adding depth and detail as you work, using paintbrushes of different sizes for varying effects. Remember to leave the paint to dry in between stages.

Dressing the cake

1 Roll 200g (7oz) of the red sugar paste into a ring. Dampen the top of the base tier 2cm (³/₄in) inside the cake with a moistened paintbrush and fix the ring into position as shown.

2 Fill a piping bag with red royal icing and pipe a blob on the red sugar paste ring. Fix the first open rose into position at an angle to bridge the gap between the third and base tiers.

4 Fix the first black ribbon loop next to the open rose by pushing it into the sugar paste ring.

5 Add a red ribbon loop and organza ribbon loop in a similar way to fill the space, and then butt the next open rose up against the ribbons, fixed into position with royal icing.

6 Continue to work around the tier until there are no gaps.

7 Mound the remaining 50g (2oz) red sugar paste into a dome for the top tier and fix into position with a little water. Push 3 red ribbon loops into a triangular position in the dome and fix 3 red open roses between the loops with royal icing. Build up the top decoration with the remaining ribbon loops. Use the sharp scissors to snip the ribbon loop tails at a nice angle to complete the decoration.

Strawberry Squares

Try these pretty, hand-painted strawberry squares as an introduction to hand painting. Choose a vanilla-flavoured cake filled with strawberry conserve and vanilla buttercream for the perfect summer picnic cake.

You will need (per cake):
- 4cm (1½in) individual square cake (see p.66 for cutting instructions)
- 60g (2½oz) marzipan, sugar paste or white chocolate plastique, for the base coat
- 75g (3oz) blue sugar paste (see p.68), for the top coat
- 20cm (8in) green-and-white striped ribbon, 7mm (⅜in) wide

Plus:
- royal icing, for fixing
- red, greens, yellow and white colour dusts
- cocoa butter

Equipment:
- piping bag
- tracing paper and fine-liner pen
- non-toxic pencil
- selection of paintbrushes, from medium to fine

Preparing the cakes
Cover each cake with a base coat of your choice, as shown on pp.66–7, and the blue sugar paste top coat, as shown on p.68. Leave to dry overnight. Surround the cakes with the green and white ribbon, and fix into position with a dab of royal icing.

Decorating the cakes
1 Trace the strawberry template on p.214 and transfer the design onto the top of each cake, using a non-toxic pencil. Be careful not to press too hard, or else the icing will crack.

2 Prepare a saucer, with the colour dusts around the edge and the cocoa butter in the middle, suspended over a bowl of simmering water. Mix the colours with the butter. Begin by painting the base red strawberry colour onto each cake. Leave to dry. Add the green strawberry calyx and stalk for each cake, building up different colours of greens to create a sense of depth.

3 To finish, add the fine yellow detail to each strawberry using the finest brush.

Love Birds

This cake gives you the opportunity to combine two techniques: a hand-painted design contained within a gilded frame, which has additional lustred hand piping. The cake would also work well with hand-painted flowers, a favourite animal or pet or an urn of fresh, tumbling fruits.

Preparing the cake

Place the cake on the cake board and cover with a base coat of your choice, as shown on p.71, and the sugar paste top coat, as shown on p.72. Line the base board with white sugar paste, as shown on p.73. Surround the base board with the 15mm (⅝in) gold ribbon, fixed with glue, and the cake with the 25mm (1in) gold ribbon, fixed with a dab of royal icing. Leave the cake and base board to dry overnight.

Decorating the cake

1 Fix the cake centrally into position on the base board with royal icing. Trace the template on p.212 and transfer onto the top of the cake at an angle, as shown, using a non-toxic pencil.

2 Place ½ tsp of each colour dust around the edge of a china saucer suspended over a saucepan of simmering water, and place the cocoa butter in the centre to melt. Mix the colours for the birds, as required. Use the paintbrushes to begin painting the love birds, building up the base layers. Use the gold lustre blended with cocoa butter to paint the frame and the crown.

3 Paint the final details with a very fine paintbrush, and leave to set.

4 Fit the piping bag with the nozzle and fill with gold royal icing. Pressure pipe the pearl design on either side of the frame. Fill the rim of the frame and the crown with pearls, and also add some pearls at each corner of the cake, just above the ribbon. Leave to set for 1 hour. Mix the gold lustre and dipping alcohol together and brush the liquid over all the pearls to finish.

You will need:
- 15cm (6in) square cake
- 15cm (6in) thick square cake board
- marzipan, sugar paste or white chocolate plastique, for the base coat (see pp.71 and 72 for quantity)
- white sugar paste, for the top coat and base board (see p.72 for quantities)
- 23cm (9in) square base board
- 95cm (38in) gold ribbon, 15mm (⅝in wide)
- 70cm (28in) gold ribbon, 25mm (1in) wide
- 1 quantity gold royal icing (see pp.77–8)
- colour dusts in yellow, pink, greens, white, blush, black and brown
- 5–6 cocoa butter buttons
- ½ tsp gold lustre
- 1 tsp dipping alcohol

Equipment:
- glue stick
- tracing paper, fine-liner pen and non-toxic pencil
- medium to fine paintbrushes
- piping bag
- no. 2 icing nozzle

True Blue

This delicate design expertly combines hand painting, hand piping and run-outs to create a beautiful wedding cake. The top tier has painted initials surrounded with delicate butterflies, run-out flowers and hand-piped pearls to create a découpage effect. A central column has been used to separate the top two tiers, thus elongating the cake. This design would transpose perfectly to a single-tier cake.

You will need:

- 10cm (4in), 15cm (6in), 20cm (8in) and 25cm (10in) round cakes
- 10cm (4in), 15cm (6in), 20cm (8in) and 25cm (10in) thick round cake boards
- marzipan, sugar paste or white chocolate plastique, for the base coat (see pp.71 and 72 for quantity)
- ivory sugar paste (see p.68), for the top coat and base board (see p.72 for quantities)
- 33cm (13in) round base board
- 16 dowelling rods
- 3.6m (12ft) ivory ribbon, 15mm (5/8in) wide
- 1 quantity royal icing, divided into 2 bowls and one coloured ivory and one blue (see pp.77–8)
- 7.5cm (3in) round polystyrene block, 2.5cm (1in) deep
- 12.5cm (5in) round polystyrene block, 2.5cm (1in) deep
- 45cm (18in) ivory ribbon, 25mm (1in) wide
- 25g (1oz) cocoa butter
- blue and white colour dusts
- topaz lustre
- dipping alcohol

Equipment:

- waxed paper
- 3 piping bags
- glue stick
- tracing paper and fine-liner pen
- non-toxic pencil
- paintbrushes
- 2 no. 1.5 icing nozzles

Preparing the cake

Cut the 15cm (6in) and 25cm (10in) cakes to a depth of 5cm (2in). Place the cakes on same-size cake boards and cover with a base coat of your choice, as shown on pp.70–71, and the ivory sugar paste top coat, as shown on p.72. Line the base board with ivory sugar paste, as shown on p.73, and edge it with 15mm (5/8in) ivory ribbon. Leave the cakes and board to dry overnight.

Fix the base tier centrally into position on the base board with a dab of ivory royal icing and dowel the base tier for direct stacking, using 6 of the dowels, as shown on p.83. Surround all the tiers with 15mm (5/8in) ivory ribbon, fixed into position with a dab of royal icing. Surround both polystyrene blocks with 25mm (1in) wide ribbon, fixed into position with a glue stick.

Decorating the cake

1 Fit a piping bag with an icing nozzle and fill with some of the blue royal icing. Pipe 30 flower outlines in different sizes divided between 2 sheets of waxed paper.

2 Pipe a blue pearl in the middle of half the flowers, and set to one side.

3 Thin a little of the blue royal icing with water to flooding consistency, put it into a second piping bag and flood the remaining flowers, as shown on p.97, using a paintbrush to ease the icing into place.

4 Fit the third piping bag with the other icing nozzle and fill with ivory royal icing. Pipe an ivory pearl in the centre of each run-out flower. Leave all the flowers to dry overnight.

5

6

7

5 Trace the template of the butterflies and background flowers on p.213 and transfer onto each tier with a non-toxic pencil. Melt the cocoa butter on a saucer over a pan of simmering water and blend with the blue and white colour dusts around the edge of the saucer to get a range of different blues. Use the colour mixtures and paintbrushes to paint in the design on the tiers.

6 Using the piping bag with the ivory royal icing, pipe additional ivory detail on the butterflies.

7 Fix the lace flowers and run-out flowers into position on each tier to build up the decoration.

8 Pipe further detail on the cake as desired. Leave to dry. Mix the topaz lustre with enough dipping alcohol to form a runny liquid. Paint the ivory pearl detail with the topaz lustre for a professional finish. To assemble, dowel the second and third tiers as shown on p.83 for a central column, using 5 dowels for each tier. Fix the central columns into position with royal icing. Leave to set before stacking the tiers and presenting on a glass cake stand.

TIP
The central columns used here are the least stable of all the stacking methods, and, as such, require very careful handling. Once prepared, the cake should be assembled in its final position only for presentation. At this time, it is sensible to royal ice the tiers into position on the top of each central column. Allow time for the tier below to begin setting before proceeding with the next tier.

8

Templates

These templates cross-refer to the cakes in this book. Use tracing or greaseproof paper and a black fine-liner pen. For hand-painted designs, trace the relevant template with the pen, then turn the tracing over and place over a clean sheet of paper, so that the design shows through clearly. Trace over the back of the design with a non-toxic pencil, then trace it directly and lightly onto the surface of the cake with the pencil, leaving the impression clearly visible but avoiding denting the cake. Designs for cakes that are not hand painted should be traced with the pen and then pricked through the paper onto the cake with a pokey tool.

Honeybees p.196

Love Birds p.206

True Blue p.208

Summer Butterflies p.144

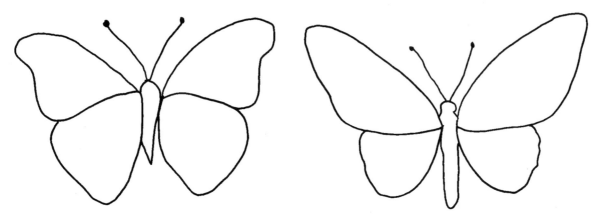

Baskets in Bloom p.146

Strawberry Squares p.204

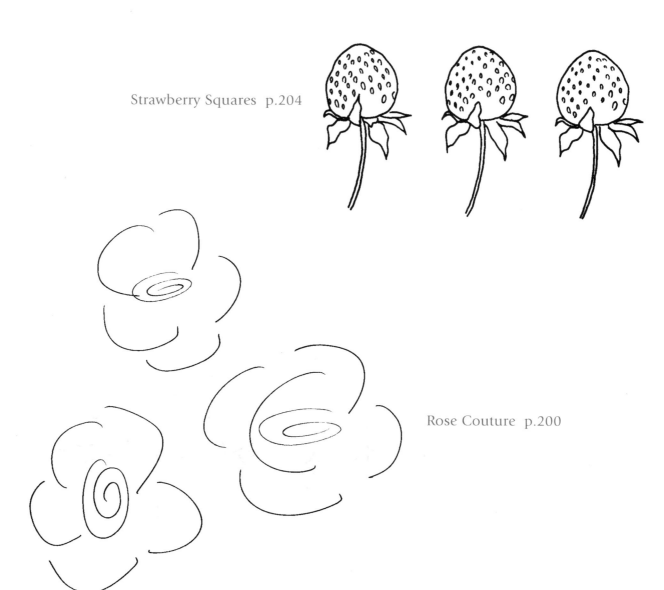

Rose Couture p.200

Passion Flower p.198

Purple Azalea Lace p.134
Georgian Lace p.142

Florence Cupcake p.172

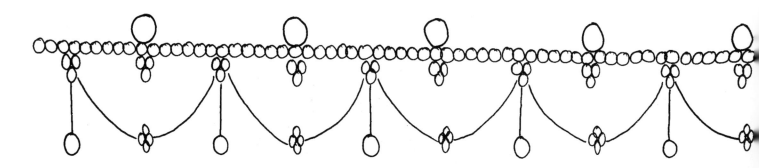

Pretty in Pink p.124

Valentine Heart p.160

Pompadour Trinkets p.138

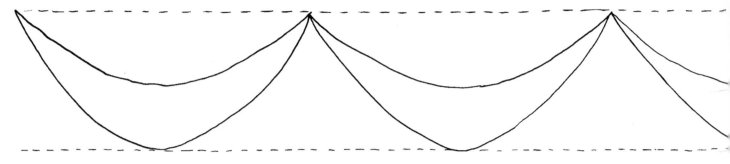

Candy Cane p.150

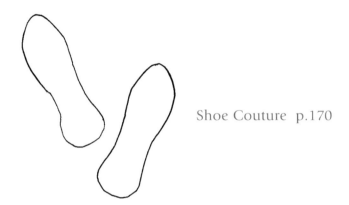

Shoe Couture p.170

Hello, Dolly! p.128

Art Nouveau p.122

Useful Addresses

Cake decorating and baking supplies

CONTINENTAL CHEF SUPPLIES
2 Swan Road
South West Industrial Estate
Peterlee
County Durham
SR8 2HS
Tel 0808 988 8981
www.chefs.net

COPPER GIFTS
Tel 1-620-421-0654
www.coppergifts.com

DIVERTIMENTI
Head Office
227–229 Brompton Road
London, SW3 2EP
Tel 0870 129 5026
www.divertimenti.co.uk

EDABLE ART
Unit 6 Coppull Enterprise Centre
Coppull
Chorley
PR7 5BW
Tel 01257 471872
www.adableart.co.uk

HOBBYCRAFT
Tel 01202 596100
www.hobbycraft.co.uk

JOHN LEWIS
300 Oxford Street
London
W1A 1EX
Tel 08456 049 049
www.johnlewis.com

KEYLINK LIMITED
Green Lane, Ecclesfield
Sheffield
S35 9WY
Tel 0114 245 5400
www.keylink.org

LAKELAND
Alexandra Buildings
Windermere
LA23 1BQ
Tel 01539 488100
www.lakelandlimited.com

LITTLE VENICE CAKE COMPANY
15 Manchester Mews
London
W1U 2DX
Tel 020 7486 5252
www.lvcc.co.uk

A PIECE OF CAKE
18–20 Upper High Street
Thame
Oxon OX9 3EX
Tel 01844 213428
www.apieceofcakethame.co.uk

SQUIRES SHOP
Squires Group
Squires House,
3 Waverley Lane,
Farnham,
Surrey
GU98BB
Tel 0845 6171 810
www.squires-shop.com

SUGAR SHACK
Tel 020 8204 2994
www.sugarshack.co.uk

SURBITON ART AND SUGARCRAFT
Tel 020 8391 4664
www.surbitonart.co.uk

TOWN & COUNTRY FINE FOODS,
Thomas Road,
Wooburn Industrial Park,
Wooburn Green,
Buckinghamshire,
HP10 0PE
Tel 01628 538000
www.tcfinefoods.co.uk

Ribbons

BARNETT LAWSON (TRIMMINGS) LTD
16–17 Little Portland Street
London
W1W 8NE
Tel 020 7636 8591
www.bltrimmings.com

MACCULLOCH & WALLIS
25-26 Dering Street
London
W1S 1AT
Tel 020 7629 0311
www.macculloch-wallis.co.uk

V V ROULEAUX
Sloane Square Shop
261 Pavilion Road
Sloane Square
SW1X 0PB
Tel 0207 627 4455
www.vvrouleaux.com

Index